YOU ABSOLUTELY COULDN'T MAKE IT UP

Jack Crossley spent some 40 years in Fleet Street, first as a reporter on the *Daily Mail* and later as news editor/assistant editor on the *Mail*, the *Observer*, the *Herald* (Glasgow), the *Daily Express*, *The Times* and, for two crazy months, the *National Enquirer* in Florida.

He also edited the *Sunday Standard*, a short-lived quality broadsheet in Scotland, and was briefly a reporter on the Quincy *Patriot Ledger* in Massachusetts.

He now lives in London, with his wife, Kate.

D1638927

You Absolutely Couldn't Make It Up

BY JACK CROSSLEY

You Absolutely Couldn't Make It Up

**MORE
HILARIOUS
BIZARRE-BUT-TRUE
STORIES FROM AROUND
BRITAIN**

JOHN BLAKE

For Jessica and Lillie

Published by John Blake Publishing Ltd,
3, Bramber Court, 2 Bramber Road,
London W14 9PB, England

www.blake.co.uk

First published in paperback in 2005

ISBN 1 84454 180 0

British Library Cataloguing-in-Publication Data:

A catalogue record for this book is available from the British Library.

Design by www.envydesign.co.uk

Illustrations by John Miers

Printed in Great Britain by BookMarque, Surrey

1 3 5 7 9 10 8 6 4 2

Papers used by John Blake Publishing are natural, recyclable
products made from wood grown in sustainable forests.
The manufacturing processes conform to the environmental
regulations of the country of origin.

Contents

Introduction

For the best part of half a century I toiled in the rich pastures of Home News for a clutch of Fleet Street papers. The Street of Adventure. The Street of Shame. Call it what you will – it was a street that produced some of the best and some of the worst newspapers in the world.

Holding my job down among the best involved starting at 6.30am – reading a daily mountain of newspapers and magazines, from the *Daily Sketch* (deceased) to the *Financial Times*, from the *Sun* to the *Wall Street Journal*, from *Private Eye* to the *Economist*.

Working through until 9pm was common. Going on until midnight was not unknown.

Some called this madness. I called it fun.

A lot of the fun – amid front page headlines on wars, disaster, scandal, crooked politicians and fraudulent fat cats – came from stumbling across the items that make up this book. I marvelled at the wonderful eccentricities of the

British and spent almost as much time hunting down the bizarre and the barmy as I did seeking out exclusive splashes.

Hence another collection of hilarious, yet true, stories devoted to Britain's peculiarities. It is pleasing to see this series benefiting from the renewed interest shown in our language and our character. I also enjoy the fact that the growing army of *You Couldn't Make It Up* fans gets pleasure in half-inching my stuff and spreading it across the world on the Net!

Perhaps you would like to join in. Can you spot a funny tale in your favourite newspaper? If so, send it along to John Blake Publishing and there'll be a bottle of something sparkling for the best entry.

Jack Crossley
September 2005

Chapter 1

Best of Britishness

Arrogant, rain-sodden, narrow-minded, old-fashioned, rude, narrow-minded, not very sexy, white-skinned toffs. Meet the British...

My parents moved into a relatively genteel, terrace street in Abingdon in 1946, five doors down from two maiden sisters. In 1954 they received a written invitation to tea from the sisters saying: 'We do so like to make newcomers feel welcome.' Diggory Seacome, Cheltenham.

Daily Telegraph

It happens every year – temperatures go over 80°F and it's headline news. During a hot spell in June 2004 *The Times* asked: 'Which other nation manages year after year to be surprised that in winter it gets a tad cold and in the summer a little hot?' Very few consider installing air conditioning because 'Englishmen, like mad dogs, prefer to sweat in the midday sun. It gives them something to talk about.'

Arrogant, rain-sodden, narrow-minded, old-fashioned, white-skinned pacifist toffs. Meet the British as seen through the eyes of American teenagers surveyed by the British Council. But most of the students polled could not name the four components of the United Kingdom and one said: 'I don't think they kill each other as much as we do.'

The Times

Rude, narrow-minded, not very sexy and the food is rubbish. Meet the British as seen through a *Reader's Digest* poll in 19 European countries. But at least they thought that we had the best sense of humour.

The Times

The Europeans polled by *Reader's Digest* also thought that Britain had contributed more to the world than anyone else – 'although this seems based on our invention of football, not our great feats of discovery, adventure and exploration'.

The Times

The *Apologist* website quickly had 200,000 hits from apologetic people – including one saying sorry for putting mice through the letterbox of a boyfriend who had dumped her and another from a waiter who put a bogey in Lady Thatcher's food. 'This is Britain,' reported the *Daily Telegraph*, 'where people apologise to lamp posts after bumping into them.'

A *Financial Times* report on publisher Dorling Kindersley in 1993 revealed that in America its most successful books were the *Ultimate Sex Guide* and *The Magic of Sex*. Its bestseller in Britain was *The Royal Horticultural Society Encyclopaedia of Gardening*.

Daily Telegraph

Asked what are the most distinctive symbols of being British, respondents to a survey sponsored by Tanqueray gin put roast beef and fish and chips as joint favourites. The Queen had to settle for third place. Drinking tea was tenth, going down the pub 20th, talking about the weather 21st. Drinking gin and tonic was a lowly 87th.

The Times

Leading anthropologist Kate Fox wrote a book revealing the hidden rules of Englishness (*Watching the English*). The *Daily Mail* printed a lengthy review, including these extracts:

3

- Egg and chips are relatively classless if eaten on their own, but working class if eaten together.
- When a woman asks for back bacon I call her madam. When she calls for streaky I call her dear. (A shopkeeper quoted by Jilly Cooper) An Englishman, even if he is alone, forms an orderly queue of one.
- It is considered entirely normal for commuters to journey with the same people for years without exchanging a word.
- The most truly eccentric dresser is the Queen, who pays no attention to fashion. Because she is the Queen, people call her style 'classic' and 'timeless' rather than eccentric or weird.

An international poll by Mori attempted to pin down some of the perceptions that people have of the British. Many thought that Brits were clever, witty, had a bulldog spirit and a high regard for tradition. During discussion groups the same words came up again and again: Reserved. Uptight. Snobbish. A US view included: 'Britons are better dressed than Americans, but they've got bad teeth and are conceited.'

Guardian

The English are completely mad with their pets. It's not unusual for police forces to be mobilised to save a cat or dog from drowning. French writer Agnes Catherine Poirer in her book *Les Nouveaux Anglais*.

Daily Mail

Next day the *Daily Telegraph* reported that Fireman Doug Little saved a hamster with the kiss of life in a smoke-filled flat in Portsmouth.

Agnes Poirer's book also suggests that British society – including the upper class – is almost entirely reliant on alcohol and complains that in too many pubs the food comes straight from the microwave after days in the freezer. 'Unremarkable wines are the norm.' But, without doubt, the British are still the funniest, particularly about sex, which is complicated, clumsy and tortuous.

Daily Mail

The *Guardian's* coverage of the Poirer book quotes her on the British being the kings of eccentricity: 'devotees of the queue, ardent monarchists, fanatical darts players, weather obsessives, and eaters of toast with baked beans in tomato sauce.'

The British have decided to ignore bad weather. Men go blithely off to work in a short-sleeved shirt when it's a damp 10°C, or in a jacket when its 5°C. When the sun does come out, they take their clothes off in a few

seconds, roll down the tops of their convertibles and make a dash for the first pavement café they see... even if the sunny spell occurs in the middle of January and lasts just half an hour.

Guardian

Half the world was up all night waiting for the 2004 US presidential election result, but something more important was keeping Brits awake. A fire at the Branston factory was threatening supplies of the nation's favourite pickle. Along with its coverage of the historic US election, the *Daily Express* devoted most of page 7 to 'The Great Pickle Panic' and reported: 'Fire sparks eBay auction at £50 for a jar of Branston.'

Earlier the *Daily Mail* had devoted a whole page to the great Branston pickle disaster, asking: 'How will we cope without this national treasure?' But it did admit that the pickle was not to everyone's taste. 'There are those who would rather eat tarmac,' it admitted.

Another traditional British addiction is the soft drink Vimto. The Bird family in Cheshire have a subterranean tank of the stuff buried in their garden. A series of pipes carries the nectar into the kitchen where it is available on tap. Clive Bird, his wife Mandy and their two sons, Daniel, 12 and Tom, 9, drink around 25 pints a week.

Manchester News Online/Independent on Sunday

The *Guardian* said it was a peculiarly British affair. The *Telegraph* regarded it as British sang-froid at its most alluring. This was the story of the P&O luxury world cruise that never got further than the Isle of Wight, due to engine trouble on the *Aurora*. Having spent 11 days of January 2005 stuck in Southampton, it would not have been unreasonable for passengers to utter a word or two of complaint. Instead they said things like 'Mustn't grumble' and spoke proudly of 'the Dunkirk spirit' when the cruise was finally abandoned.

Perhaps 11 days of free drinking and dining and a full refund helped. Passengers on the *Aurora* got through 12,626 bottles of wine and champagne, 12,843 bottles of beer, 1,246 bottles of spirits and 9,800 cocktails.

The DK Eyewitness Travel Guide to Great Britain assures foreigners that afternoon tea, taken at around 4pm, is a British tradition enacted daily in homes, teashops and grand hotels. (The same guide says that 'long periods of adverse weather are rare' here and that the railway system is generally efficient.)

The Times

A humble cup of tea is joining the Magna Carta and Hadrian's Wall on a government website celebrating great British cultural icons. This inspired the *Daily Express* to run a page devoted to tea, which included the items:

- 'Tea for two' was an 18th-century street vendor's cry, offering a pot of tea for twopence.
- George Orwell, author of *1984*, described tea as one of the mainstays of civilisation and devised 11 tea rules. They included: 'Don't add creamy milk,' 'add milk to the tea, not vice versa.' and 'no sugar'.
- 'Never trust a man who, when left alone in a room with a tea cosy, doesn't try it on.' Billy Connolly.

My mother was asked by an American to explain the differences in the various types of tea she had come across in Britain: afternoon tea, high tea, cream tea, meat tea and just 'tea'. Mother thought she had explained quite well until the American asked: 'And do you British eat them all every day?' Jenny M. Gorsuch, Little Chalfont, Buckinghamshire.

The Times

The quintessentially British preoccupation of enjoying a biscuit with a nice cup of tea has now got its own website called nicecupofteaandasitdown.com. It is a surprise hit on the Internet, having attracted 250,000 followers. Stuart Payne, 40, an information

technology consultant in Cambridge, started the
website 'as a bit of joke' and discovered that 'there is
a kind of reverence for biscuits because they are part
of British life.'

Daily Telegraph

**Mr Payne's website reviews packets of biscuits as
though they were fine wines or rare malt whiskies.
Among biscuit-nibblers, the great dilemma is whether to
dunk or not to dunk. He says Rich Tea are the best for
dunking, but admits that there are those who regard
dunking as being in bad taste.**

The Times

Mr Payne's choice of dunkworthy biscuits was not
backed up by a team of food scientists – they
crowned the ginger nut as the best option for the
cognoscenti. After laboratory experiments, they
reported that, when dunked, the ginger biscuit
becomes more gingery and holds its crunch. Ideal
dunking time: 2.92 seconds.

Guardian

**There's no sign of a truce in the North v South war. In the
row over plans to relocate thousands of civil servants up
North one of them said: 'I'd defy anyone to give me one
good reason why I should move out of London to some
grim, northern hell-hole.' Northerner Brian Reade, in his
Daily Mirror column turned up his own 20 good reasons.**

They included:

- It doesn't take three hours to get to work.
- There's no congestion, let alone a charge.
- Strangers talk to you.
- You can afford to live in something bigger than a shoe-box for under £300,000.
- When your boiler breaks men come and fix it.

The reputation of the Scots as dour and miserable has been reinforced by academic research. A study by a network of university economists indicates that Scots have remained steadfastly miserable for 30 years while others in Britain have grown happier. Nevertheless, Scots ranked happier than some Europeans, including the Germans.

Daily Telegraph

The *Daily Telegraph* intro on the story above was: 'P.G. Wodehouse's remark that "it is never difficult to distinguish between a Scotsman with a grievance and a ray of sunshine" appears still to hold true.'

Britons are among the most dishonest people in the world. In a survey by the University of Manchester a high percentage of British consumers said it was OK to:

- Change price tags in stores.

- Consume a can of drink in a supermarket and not pay for it.
- Take towels from hotels.
- Rent a double room and use it for more than two people.
- Report a lost item as stolen to an insurance company.
- Not say anything when charged too little.

The survey was published in the *Journal of Consumer Marketing* and covered Europe, Asia and America. It reported: 'When it comes to basic ethics we fall well behind standards in the USA.'

Independent on Sunday

Maybe its because I'm a Londoner that I love London so – but that doesn't stop me knowing hardly anything about it. In a survey one in five people shown a picture of the South Bank against the London skyline thought it was Sydney. One in four thought that a shot of the river at Richmond was a photograph of the Amazon. More than half believed that a picture of Regent Street was Italy. On average Londoners did no better than people from elsewhere in the country.

The Times

Any excuse to reminisce about the bowler hat is still seized upon by the British press. An old photograph in *The Times* of two men wearing them brought a flurry of nostalgic letters:

- Guards officers in their 'civvies' wore bowler hats and were so easily recognised that they were sometimes saluted in the streets around Whitehall or Birdcage Walk.
- It may now seem to be outdated, but what an astonishing creation it was. Invented in 1851 and manufactured by the Bowler factory in south London, its early use was as a servant's hat.
- It was worn by royalty in the 1880s and then by businessmen. Building site foremen wore them to signify status.

D.W.S. Gray of Newcastle upon Tyne provided the above information and then added that he can no longer wear his own bowler on the street because of the numbers of older people 'who approach me to discuss it with elegiac resignation'.

The Times

The above was followed a few days later with:

- My grandfather told me that foremen in Belfast shipyards wore bowler hats not only as a mark of status but also as protection

from dropped rivets, accidental and
otherwise. C.H. Emeleus, Durham, *The Times*

- The bowler remained a special item of
working class headgear until at least the late
1950s. My wife's grandfather, an ex-miner,
kept one to wear at funerals, in place of his
cloth cap. John Acklaw, *Essex Times*

After the think tank Demos said that trainspotters, stamp collectors and other geeks, nerds and anoraks promote social cohesion, Stephen O'Loughlin, of Huddersfield, reminded readers that the French philosopher Montesquieu had held that the British had never had a revolution because they spent too much time on their hobbies.

Daily Telegraph

Shock! Horror! True Brits reacted predictably when the story broke that Blackpool was talking about getting rid of its deckchairs because of their 'flat cap' image. Mayor Maxine Callow said: 'The deckchair is part of Blackpool's seaside heritage.' Deckchair operators said: 'They've been on Blackpool beach since 1914 and some of the ones we've got are 40 years old. We hired deckchairs to 70,000 punters last year and each year you see the same faces. They even put their chairs on the same spots on the beach.'

Sun

The *Guardian's* coverage revealed that one of Blackpool's deckchairs is a joke one, which is impossible to erect.

Immigrants are to be tested on the customs that are central to British life. A government handbook to help them settle in includes:

- Details of Father Christmas, but not of Winston Churchill. (Santa 'is a cheerful old man with a beard who travels on a sledge pulled by reindeer delivering presents to children.')
- The ingredients of Christmas pudding.
- The importance of pubs. Along with instructions on how to buy a round of drinks, the migrants are told that 'Bar staff will try to serve those who have been waiting longest' and 'If you spill a stranger's drink by accident. it is good manners (and prudent) to offer to buy another.'
- And if you want to know the time, ask a policeman. 'Police officers in the United Kingdom are protectors of the public and are expected to be friendly and helpful to anyone who seeks their assistance.' *The Times*

When faced with the vexed problem of what to do to repel a burglar, it is not very English to wield a baseball bat. Professor Paul D. Buisseret, of Chichester, West Sussex, writes: 'Let us hear no more transatlantic babble of baseball bats... Surely we should advise people of a nervous disposition to keep a cricket bat next to their beds... Remember we are Englishmen.' The professor goes on to say that the Scots could always repel intruders by playing their bagpipes.

Independent

As this book is dedicated to the bizarre antics of the British, it is overjoying to learn that the Americans seem to share in the fun. Jemma Lewis, writing in the *Sunday Telegraph* from the US, says: 'I suddenly realised that almost all the British news I had heard since I got to New York had been about what utter buffoons we are. The only Brits that make it in the news here are lunatics, fox hunters, sexual miscreants, members of the Royal Family and incompetent toffs. Tony Blair's visit to Washington passed almost unnoticed – yet Boris Johnson's sexual embarrassments merited a big splash in the New York Times... Boris fits the most loveable of English stereotypes – posh, shambolic, clever, prone to mishap and a self-deprecator of genius.'

Many Europeans see the British as beer-swilling, tabloid-reading, crazy sports fans. But a survey for the Touring Club Italiano found that the British go to more concerts, films, plays, galleries and libraries than almost anyone in Europe.

Guardian

Stephen Fry won a contest to appear in a Red Nose charity edition of *The Archers* after quipping that the programme was 'the only important reason I have for living in Britain.'

Edinburgh Evening News/Daily Telegraph

Not everyone is as deeply in love with *The Archers* as Mr Fry. Helen Rumbelow, writing in the 'Thunderer' column of *The Times*, says that when the Sunday omnibus of the world's longest-running radio soap begins 'my face twists into an agonised scream and the race for the off button begins.' She says she suffers from 'the Grundies', a condition caused by any contact with Radio 4's unfeasibly popular soap. The theme tune is officially described as a maypole dance, but 'you would flinch at hearing it once at a Morris dance festival. When played more than 20 times a week, for 55 years, it becomes seriously dangerous stuff.'

Chapter 2

Signs of the Times

For Sale: Artificial leg (left). Suit tallish person with right leg only...

Warning label on a toilet brush: 'Do not use for personal hygiene'. And on a thermometer: 'Once used rectally, should not be used orally'.

Independent on Sunday

'Parachute for sale. Only used once. Never opened. Small stain. £199 ono.' Spotted in *Friday Ad*, Bournemouth, by Steve Creasy, Weymouth, Dorset.

Instructions on a push-up deodorant stick: 'Remove cap and push up bottom.'

Daily Mirror

'Weight Watchers will meet at the Presbyterian Church. Please use the large double doors.

Walkern Journal

Sign seen by Diane Gardner, of Tintagel, on a garden wall in Trewarmett, Cornwall: 'Slow Down For Fox Sake'.
Daily Mail

The instructions for my steam iron include: 'Do not use on any clothing while being worn. Remove the item of clothing, iron it, then allow to cool before wearing it again'.

Catherine Donker, Bath, *The Times*

'Mirror, unused, £20'. Classified ad spotted by C. J. O'Connor of Swansea in the *South Wales Evening Post*.

Sign at Gatwick Airport: 'Your nearest alternative toilet is located on this level – towards the spectators' viewing facility'. Mary Scarborough, Hastings.

Daily Mail

G.E. Pinkerton, of Huntingdon, bought a small Japanese motorcycle for his son. Its manual gave instructions for using the electric and kick starters and, if both failed, how to run with the bike in gear and then engage the clutch. 'Should this fail repeat until the engine fires or until the destination is reached.'
The Times

'Wasps nests destroyed £20. OAPs £15'. Sign seen by Barbara Taylor of Bristol. *Yours* magazine

Sign on a farmer's gate: 'Please shut gate to stop sheep worrying.'
Nicholas Grace, Overton, Hampshire, *Independent*

Passengers to wait ten years for fast trains.
Times headline

Twelve-year wait for toilets.
***Long Eaton Advertiser* headline**

Roger Craig of Otley, West Yorkshire, complained in *The Times* that his new digital camera (described as 'easy to use') came with a 156-page operating manual that was larger and heavier than the camera.

Sign on arts centre entrance in Warrington: 'Push Button To Open Automatic Doors'.
Seen by C. Law of Weaverham, Cheshire, *Daily Mail*

Residents of the village of Willey, near Bridgnorth in Shropshire, got fed up of pranksters stealing their road signs. So they stopped having signs bearing just the word 'Willey' and put up ones saying 'Willey Village'. The thieving stopped.
Sun

Seen by Jonathan Morse of Bristol in the town of Woodbine, Georgia: 'Dead Peoples' Things For Sale'.

Daily Mail

People who complain about the complexities of flat-pack furniture may take heart from the following instructions for a cuckoo clock:

'Draw out the bellows with much circumspection... move the iron-wire or the pack thread fixed on the chain. If the clock no strike correct open the small door on the right side and press the visible wire. If the clock march too quick push the sheave for the pendulum more upwards. If the clock march too slow push the sheave more downwards.' This letter was published in *The Times* on 5 May 1936 and republished on 5 May 2004 as one of the newspaper's Past Letters to the Editor.

Sign at a supermarket in Hemel Hempstead: 'NO PARKING – Parking here may result in a £25 fixed penalty.' And underneath it: '*Always* happy to help.'

Nick Fifield, Berkhamsted, Herts, *Daily Mail*

In Manchester during the 1930s the city's trams had this notice: 'Spitting strictly prohibited'. Juxtaposed was this notice: 'Use the Ship Canal'.

Roy Powell, Selby, North Yorkshire.

Independent

Bureaucracy gone mad? Notice on the men's toilet in H.M. Treasury building in Riverside Walk: 'Evacuation Procedure'.

C. G. Brancen, London SW13, *Independent*

Sign at the entrance to Hessle Cemetery, East Yorkshire: 'One way system in operation'. Colin Watson, Hessle.

Daily Mail

Two signs on a high wall in North East England: 'Convent of Mercy' and 'Trespassers will be prosecuted.'

Margaret MacIver, Killin, Perthshire, *Independent*

The *Daily Telegraph* ran a series of readers' letters on bizarre book titles. Among them were:

- *The Art of Faking Exhibition Poultry* by G. Riley Scott, of London and published by my father, T. Werner Laurie in 1934. From Dick Laurie, London SW.
- Penny Fenn Clark, of Rochester, Kent, possesses 'a copy of my grandfather's book *Truncheons – Their Romance and Reality* by Erland Fenn Clark, 1935. 'It is a comprehensive account of a huge range of historic coshes and bludgeons and it is dedicated "To my dear wife".'

21

Seen on a building site in Hastings, Sussex: a notice with an arrow pointing upwards saying: 'Danger. Workmen Overhead.' Alongside is a notice with an arrow pointing downwards saying: 'Men Drinking Tea'.

Ray Cooper, London SE6, *Daily Mail*

'Special offer – Pack of six geraniums. Usually £2. Now £1.99.'

Advertisement in the *Edinburgh Evening News*

The sign identifying the village of Lost in Aberdeenshire got stolen so many times by tourists that the council announced a plan to change the village's name. But the international outcry was so huge that officials agreed that Lost would not be lost.

The Times

Sign on a van seen in Elvington, North Yorkshire: 'CAUTION! Blind man driving'. The van belongs to Grimsby Sunblinds. David Spark, Bramhope, Leeds.

Daily Mail

'Dentures as new. One tooth missing in top front, slightly discoloured – hence £5. No offers.'

Classified ad in *Lancashire Evening Telegraph*

Devon County Council Education Committee advertised for part-time domestic help and specified: 'Good scrubber preferred.' Seen in a 1957

edition of the *Exmouth Journal* by Valerie and
Trevor Morgan, Exmouth, Devon.

**'Blind applicants may request further details on audio
tape.' Advert for relief drivers in the *Rugby Advertiser***

The tiny hamlet of Whitwell on the north side of
Rutland Water has a proud notice: 'Whitwell –
Twinned with Paris.' I do not know if Paris displays
'Twinned with Whitwell' on its name plates.
                                Robert Tee, Leeds, *Guardian*

**My understanding is that Whitwell parish council wrote
to the mayor of Paris stating that it wished to twin with
the city and would assume – unless told otherwise – that
this would be welcomed.**
            Joseph Hickis, Blandford Forum, Dorset, *Guardian*

My new electric patio heater arrived with a 12-page
manual containing valuable safety instructions
including: 'This heater is hot when in use.'
                Miles McInnes, Penrith, Cumbria, *The Times*

**Seen under a 'No Entry' sign at Chessington World of
Adventure in Surrey: 'Private Parts. Access to staff only.'
        Russell Davies of Worthing, West Sussex, *Daily Mail***

Mrs M. Lawler, of Shipston on Stour, Warwickshire,
spotted this notice on a blackboard giving information

about the electric train service up to the top of Snaefell mountain on the Isle of Man: 'Next Car Departs – Every Now and Then – Unless Full Before'.

Daily Mail

Sign in an antique shop in Tetbury, Wiltshire: 'Sale of Old Stock'.

Seen by Mike Saxton of Chelmsford.

Road sign seen in West Dorset by Clair Saxby of Epsom:

> # BRADPOLE
> Please arive carefull rough village

Daily Mail

Ad in the *Herald Express*, Torbay: 'Delightful two-bed apartment in desirable location. Grade 2 listing building.'

Dominic Greyer has spent years photographing road signs bearing the most peculiar place names in Britain. One hundred and twenty of them appear in his book *Far From Dull and Other Places*. The *Daily Mail* made a two-page spread from a selection of the signs. They included:

- Dull in Perthshire
- Drinkers End in Worcestershire

- **Chipshop in Devon**
- **Brawl in Scotland**
- **Ogle in Northumberland**
- **Crackpot in North Yorkshire**
- **Seething in Norfolk**
- **Lover in Wiltshire**

The sign for Bedlam near Harrogate has 'Please Drive Carefully' underneath the name. The sign for Old, in Northamptonshire has 'Please Drive Slow'.

D. Johnson of Watford, Herts, saw this Derby County Football club ad for hospitality packages: 'Match ticket with private balcony seating, three course carvery/four course silver service, full-time and half-time refreshments, reserved car parking, private bar facility, full use of a Derby County hostess.'

Daily Mail

Road sign seen in Wootton Bassett, Wilts, by George Anderson of Swindon:

'HUMPED
ZEBRA
CROSSING' *Daily Mail*

Condor Blended pipe tobacco carries the health warning: 'Smoking when pregnant harms your baby.'

Sunday Telegraph

In November 1989 the *Guardian* began publishing a feature called 'Notes & Queries' and it still thrives on a diet of the bizarre, the trivial and the perverse. On 17 November 2004 the paper celebrated 15 years of N&Q and published a selection of some of the best exchanges. This is one of the Queries:

Can anyone confirm that somewhere in a field in the north of England there used to be a sign saying 'Please do not throw stones at this notice'? Are there other examples of this kind of helpful public information?

These are just two of the Notes which followed:

Printed on toilet paper tissues at the Harwell Laboratories in the 1970s: 'Not for resale'.

Outside Shap Abbey in Cumbria: 'Admission Free. Special terms for parties'.

'Retired, professional widower, seeks relationship with view to marriage.' Personal ad in *Yours* magazine, spotted by Mrs M. Windscheffel, Norwich.

Daily Mail

In Bridgnorth, Shropshire – an estate agent called Doolittle and Dalley.

Daily Telegraph

In Leamington Spa, a solicitors firm called Wright Hassall.
Daily Telegraph

In Leicester – Dentith & Dentith, Dental Surgeons.

Daily Telegraph

In Twickenham – a firm of funeral directors called Wake and Paine.

Daily Telegraph

'Dog Fouling – it's in your hands.'

Headline in the *Exeter Citizen*

'Tanning – Full body spray £25 – plus get a friend spayed for half price.'

Spotted in the *South Manchester Reporter* by Roy Wadsworth, Manchester

Spotted by Paul Feltham of Hastings at an Indian restaurant: Notice: 'No Cash Kept on Premises. Overnight Take Away Service Available'.

Daily Mail

UK tourists write to Thomas Cook about the hilarious signs they spot on their holidays:

- At the laundry: 'Ladies, leave your clothes here and spend the afternoon having a good time.'
- At the dry cleaners: 'Drop your trousers here for the best results.'
- At the hotel: 'Because of the impropriety of

entertaining guests of the opposite sex in the
bedroom, it is suggested that the lobby be
used for this purpose.' *Sun*

Amid the row over banning smoking in pubs and
other public places, Rodney Legg, of Wincanton, tells
of the Virginia Ash pub at Henstridge, Somerset,
which has a sign showing a servant throwing a
bucket of water over a smoker. The smoker getting a
drenching is Sir Walter Raleigh who lived nearby.

The Times

'Disabled Entrance. If locked enquire within.' Spotted
on the door of a pub on Portland Bill.

John Dewdney, Poole, Dorset, *Daily Mail*

'Fat, lazy old cob required for fat, lazy old man who
wishes to go hunting now that it is illegal.'
Ad in the *North Devon Journal* spotted by Sarah
Powell of Bideford, Devon.

Notice at the Mayflower Centre in Plymouth: 'Please do
not sit on the seating. Thank You.' Spotted by David
Hanson of Exeter.

Daily Mail

Sign outside a school in Chester: 'No Parking In
Front of Gates Or In Car Park. Thank You.'
Spotted by Gordon Stockley of Chester, *Daily Mail*

Notice at a West Sussex nursery school: 'We have had a case of head lice. Please check your child's hair regularly. Girls with long hair need to be tied up.'

Susan Mortimer, Selsey, West Sussex, *Reader's Digest*

'For Sale – Small white pups, mother Jack Russell type, father came through catflap, £15.'

Ad in the *Taunton, Wellington and Minehead Scan* (November 1989)

Allan Proud of Perthshire spotted this name sign on a solicitors' office in Ireland: Argue & Phibbs.

Daily Mail

A card in a post office window in West Jesmond, Newcastle carried this message: 'Found. Brown and white hamster. Apply within. (Sorry it is dead.)'

Daily Telegraph

'Hark! The herald angel sins.' Spotted on Liskeard carol service hymn sheet in Cornwall by Andy Frost, Callington, Cornwall.

Daily Mail

Sign on the wall of gents lavatory in Weymouth, Dorset: 'In an emergency phone coastguard Weymouth 4105'.

Spotted by D. Jones of Hornchurch, Essex.

Daily Mail

Avon & Somerset police recommend using WD40 in lavatories to stop people snorting cocaine. If the colourless oil is sprayed onto flat surfaces it congeals and semi-dissolves the drug.

Evening Standard

Newspaper billboard spotted by Mrs M. Stephens, of Chesham, Bucks:

EXAMINER
Chesham
Thieves Raid
High Street
Shop Every
Thursday

Warning on the infant medicine being given to the eight-month-old daughter of Mark Leneve, of Romsey, Hampshire: 'May cause drowsiness. If affected do not drive or operate machinery. Avoid alcoholic drink.'

Daily Mail

'Artificial leg (left) with matching shoe (left). Only walked two miles. Suit tallish person with right leg only. £65 ono.'

Ad spotted in *Scoop*, by Julia and Barry Dunlinson, St Leonards on Sea, East Sussex, *Daily Mail*

Sign on the door of a Chinese restaurant: 'CLOSED. Kitchen on Fire'.

> Spotted by Mike Nourse and Alex Newbury,
> of Southsea, Hampshire, *Daily Mail*

'Sexual abuse centre looking for volunteers'.

> Headline seen in *Esher News* by Moya Fry,
> Long Ditton, Surrey, *Daily Mail*

Tesco's slogan 'Every little helps' appears on the door of the ladies toilet in a store visited by Karen Sadler, of Bristol. 'I did my best. I hope it was appreciated,' she writes in the *Independent*.

Guy Swillingham's book *The Best of the Worst in British Shop Names* features examples of storefront comedy including:

- Junk and Disorderly – a removals and house clearance firm in West London.
- Jack the Stripper – door and furniture strippers in Twickenham.
- Pane in the Glass – window sales in Ashford, Surrey.
- Get Laid Professionally – carpet showroom in Consett, Co. Durham.
- Criminal Records – second-hand record shop in Tunbridge Wells. *Sun*

Advert in a catalogue for a computer workstation: 'Supplied flat-packed with instructions for self-assembly. Allow five working days.'

Spotted by John Morse of Olney, Buckinghamshire.
Daily Mail

Seen in a Bolton store by R. Young of Bolton: 'Toilet Tissue 92p. Ass colours.'

Daily Mail

A *Times* reader pondered on a toilet cleaner's claim to 'kill 99.9 per cent of all known germs' and asked: 'What happens to the rest?' Another reader responded: 'The average dishcloth is said to harbour some 15 billion germs. After 99.9 per cent have been killed, it will still have 15 million of the blighters.'

Local paper advert spotted by Lance Jenkins, Hertfordshire: 'Burwash, East Sussex. Detached executive home, four bedrooms, lounge, dining room, spacious kitchen/breakfast room and separate downstairs toilet. No chain.'

Daily Mail

'People wishing to send written complaints and comments to First North Western are invited to address them to their customer liaison manager, Ashley Grumble.'

Notice spotted by H.A. Dransfield, Manchester.
Daily Mail

Chapter 3

What's up, Doc?

Pigeon droppings will cure baldness...

Answers to a questionnaire asking patients why they required transport to and from a chiropody clinic included:

- 'I am under the doctor and cannot breathe.'
- 'My husband cannot bring me. He is dead.'
- 'If mother goes out alone she gets into trouble.'
- 'When you bring me back, will you drop me off at the White Swan?' Mrs D. Pepperell, Lichfield, Staffs. *Daily Mail*

A patient diagnosed as clinically depressed was scheduled for controversial shock therapy until it was discovered he was not depressed – merely Scottish. BBC *News Quiz*

Rumpole creator John Mortimer, 81, writes: 'A doctor asked me if I felt breathless when taking exercise. "How would I know?" I replied. "I've never taken any."'

The Times magazine

"Thirty-nine people a year visit UK hospital emergency clinics after accidents involving tea cosies," according to a book called *Numbers* by David Boyle and Anita Roddick.

When Sir Winston Churchill was in his eighties, he had a hip operation in the King Edward VII hospital. The press were on hand to witness his return home and *Daily Mail* photographer George Little said to the great man: 'I hope I'll be here to record your 90th birthday.' Said Winston: 'I can't see any reason why you won't, my boy. You look well enough to me.' From *The Queen, Rupert & Me* by Australian journalist and author Desmond Zwar, who was working for the *Daily Mail* at the time.

A physiotherapist whose research concluded that banana skins are not slippery slipped and fell while shopping in Kent – on a banana skin.

Daily Mirror

Alongside a story saying that balding men may eventually be able to grow hair using stem cells from their skin, *The Times* recorded anti-balding recipes dating back to 1,500BC with ingredients including the blood from the neck of the Gabgu bird, horseradish, beetroot, nettles and pigeon droppings. The headline? 'Don't Try This At Home'.

Four hundred brassiere and underwear-related injuries are recorded in Britain every year. A quarter of all house fires are caused by chip pans. Almost 70,000 people are injured every year in Britain while gardening. And more people are killed annually by teddy bears than real life grizzlies. From *100 Most Dangerous Things in Everyday Life* by Laura Lee.

Daily Mail

Professor Emeritus J.F. Paynter of East Yorkshire writes to *The Times* about his worries over the possible side effects mentioned in a leaflet accompanying one of his medicines: 'coma and death'.

Times reader Martin R. Davies, of Bristol, writes of the leaflet which came with his prescribed medication. It warned of possible side effects including: dizziness, headache, feeling sick, dry tickling cough, bronchitis, runny or stuffy nose, dry mouth, loss of appetite, stomach pains, diarrhoea or constipation, jaundice, vasculitis, angina, chest pains, irregularity of heart beat, reduced circulation to hands and feet, pins and needles, muscle cramps, tiredness, weakness, hair loss, mood changes, nervousness, restlessness, shaking, confusion, disturbance of balance, sleeping problems, sensitivity of skin to light, loosening nails.

Mr Davies reports that he has courageously taken the medication and '...despite my recklessness, so far I seem to have escaped all of them. Presumably diarrhoea and constipation have fought each other to a standstill.'

Items left behind by visitors to a Stoke on Trent swimming pool last year [2003] included ten false limbs.

The Times

Lord (Roy) Hattersley apologised at the Cheltenham Festival of Literature when he could not hear a question from the audience. He explained: 'I have hearing aids that my doctor said were identical to Bill Clinton's. He said they wouldn't make me hear any better, but they would make me irresistible to 18-year-old girls. He was right in the first case – but sadly wrong in the second.'

The Times

It took ten ambulances and a helicopter to ferry the wounded to hospital from the two-day National Festival of Women's Rugby.

Daily Mail

George Daulat of Scarborough phoned 20 dentists without getting an appointment. So he pulled out three aching teeth with a pair of rusty pliers. He said: 'I bought a bottle of vodka because there's no way I would do that sober.'

Sunday Times

Valerie Holsworth, 64, of Scarborough, North Yorkshire, could not get dental treatment on the NHS – so she pulled out five teeth herself with her husband's pliers. She said: 'I get about four lagers down me and take a good mouthful of whisky before I get started.'

Daily Express

Kingston's Walking for Health project appealed for walk leaders to help people improve their health. It promised: 'Volunteers will receive resuscitation training'.

Surrey Comet

BUPA abandoned plans to hold a conference in Dublin because of the Irish anti-smoking laws – because 41 per cent of its staff were smokers.

Sunday Telegraph

Enoch Powell remembered having measles at the age of four 'because I had to give up reading the *Encyclopaedia Britannica* at the time.'

Edinburgh Evening News

An NHS hospital is to have its windows cleaned for the first time in seven years. Dr John Hughes-Games, 77, was appalled by the state of the windows at the Bristol Oncology Centre and wanted patients to be able to see the sun and the sky. He died after three weeks of treatment for leukaemia and his last wish was to leave £1,500 to have all 400 panes cleaned.

The Times

A *Daily Telegraph* reader says she was an NHS medical secretary in the 1980s when the Amstrad was introduced with its fascinating and creative spellchecker. Among its changes were: 'Your patient has been admitted to the Beresford Ward' to 'Your patient has been admitted to the Bedsore Ward' and 'I am prescribing Lofepramine three times a day' to 'I am proscribing Lovemaking three times a day'.

Maureen Sanders, Allestree, Derbyshire

An obstetrician renowned for correctly forecasting the sex of his patients' babies explained how he did it: 'I always tell the mother it will be a girl (or a boy), then write the opposite in my diary. When the mother tells

me I was wrong, I produce my diary – so I am always right.' D. Watt, Worthing.

Daily Telegraph

Staff at the University Hospital Aintree in Liverpool were initially pleased that patients and visitors seemed to be using plenty of the antiseptic handwash gel introduced to combat superbugs. Then they discovered that the gel was being used to top up drinks. It contains a good slug of ethyl alcohol.

The Times

In February 2005 *The Times* reported that Janet Warnes had waited three years for an appointment to see ear surgeon Iain Fraser at Leeds Infirmary. She turned up at the appointed date only to be told that Mr Fraser had died two years earlier.

Thousands of Britons end up in hospital after bizarre accidents involving non-powered hand tools, earthquakes, lightning strikes, poisonous plants, marine life, lawnmowers, venomous snakes, thorns, sharp leaves, flood, storms, falling out of trees, slipping on toys and choking on balloons.

BBC / *The Times*

The list of unlikely accidents is by no means exhaustive. I survived my cockatoo crash-landing and skidding to a halt across my bald head.

Graham Smithers, Norfolk, *The Times*

Following a story about the myriad of possible uses for WD40, nurse Margaret Romney, of Hildenborough, Kent, remembered being told by a middle-aged lady: 'My aunt swears by it for her rheumatism.'

Independent

Chapter 4

Driven to Distraction

Four police cars on training exercise crash on M61...

Only hours after passing her driving test Lauren Miller, 17, drove over a cliff and landed without serious injury on a Jersey beach 100ft below. As the waves of a rising tide crashed onto the beach Lauren used a mobile to ring her father from the ruins of his car. *The Times* headline: 'Hello Dad, I passed my test, but er... I've just driven off a cliff.'

A spokesman for the Association of British Drivers said: 'If you take both hands off the wheel, you haven't got a leg to stand on.'

Westmorland Gazette

The following are genuine statements from insurance forms:

- 'The guy was all over the road. I had to swerve a number of times before I hit him.'
- 'In an attempt to kill a fly, I drove into a telephone pole.'
- 'The pedestrian had no idea which direction to run, so I ran over him.'
- 'Coming home, I turned into the wrong drive and collided with a tree I don't have.'
  Reg O'Donaghue, London SE17, *Daily Mail*

Items left behind by drivers returning vehicles have included: stockings and suspenders, a shop dummy, used nappies, false teeth, a bag of fish and chips and a dead goat. *Fleet News*, which monitors the world of company cars.

David Page, 40, dug up an object in Coltishall, Norfolk. It was a sort of canister with a button on top. He accidentally pressed down the button and then feared it might be a World War II mine that would explode if he released the button. He wrapped masking tape around his thumb to keep it in place and used his mobile to raise the alarm. Police arrived, packed his arm – and the canister – in a barrel of sand and told him: 'Do not move.' Roads were cordoned off within a two-mile radius. A woman police officer said everything would be OK and

David said to her: 'You're not the one holding the bomb.' David kept the button depressed for four hours before bomb disposal experts identified the object as part of a Citroen's hydraulic suspension system. He said later: 'It sounds funny, but it was absolutely horrendous.'

Sun/Guardian/Daily Mail

Alf Newman, 68, hailed a taxi during his holiday in Jamaica and was amazed to find it was the same Nissan Sunny he had scrapped 16 years earlier in Chichester, Sussex.

Sun

It seems to be OK if you want to take your donkey for a car ride. A man who removed the front seat of his car to accommodate his donkey was taken to court in Devon – and the magistrate dismissed the case. *The Times* was so impressed that it not only carried a congratulatory leading article in October 1969 but reprinted it in 20 October 2004. The leader writer wrote: 'Drivers who do not own donkeys will be unable to celebrate this small defence of their diminishing freedom, but they should not be carried away... by installing a stuffed donkey in the back window.'

The M61 in Lancashire was blocked after a four-cars were involved in a collision. All of them were driven by policemen on a training exercise.

Sunday Telegraph

The Northumbria Safety Camera Partnership sends out fixed penalty fines to motorists caught speeding on film. In December 2004 it released a series of spectacular excuses received from drivers. They included:

- A driver who said he was afraid of being abducted by aliens after seeing a UFO
- A claim that an aircraft approaching Newcastle airport triggered the camera
- A driver who claimed he was on a mercy dash with his dying hamster
- Another who said that very severe diarrhoea forced him to speed to a lavatory
- And one who said that a violent sneeze triggered an involuntary stamp on the accelerator. *Guardian*

It's official. Women are by far the safer drivers. Home Office statistics show that men were responsible for 88 per cent of all driving offences in England and Wales in 2002. Men account for 97 per cent of dangerous driving cases, 85 per cent of careless driving convictions and 83 per cent of all speeding tickets issued. *Daily Mirror* women's editor Clare Raymon writes: 'Men are just like little boys. They should stop treating every trip to the supermarket like a Grand Prix.'

Men are psychologically programmed to be worse drivers than women, reports the Social Issues Research Centre in Oxford. As a result of their evolution from being hunter-gatherers they are programmed for targeted aggression, the thrill of the chase and a degree of lawlessness. Women's brains are programmed for nurturing instincts, making them far less aggressive.

Daily Mail

Traffic wardens rank alongside tax inspectors and estate agents as people we love to hate. When NCP, Britain's biggest parking company, launched an 'image makeover' a top executive admitted: 'I don't think we'll ever be loved'. This appeared in a story of a poster in Manchester bearing the photograph of a local traffic warden captioned: 'The fat bitch traffic warden from Mars'.

Observer

A traffic policeman whose beat covers motorways in Hertfordshire sits in the passenger seat. He has failed his driving test twice and has no driving licence.

Sunday Telegraph

Our car's operating manual has over 20 pages explaining how to work the key.

> Mrs L.M. Blows, Watersfield, West Sussex.
> *The Times*

A Ford Sierra is pictured badly crumpled after hitting a road sign in a London street. The sign reads: 'Thank You For Driving Safely'.

> *Sun*

Exactly one year to the day after a car crashed into his house in Liversedge, West Yorkshire, Gordon White, 62, returned home to find another car had demolished the front of his house. It was driven by the same man who had crashed into the house in 2003. The same recovery man turned up to sort out the smash. The same fire crew attended the accident. Said Mr White: 'I've only just finished getting the house back to how I wanted it. If I'd known it was all going to happen again I'd have chosen cheaper wallpaper.'

> *Yorkshire Post/ Daily Mail/ Sun*

Britain is considering making drink-driving offenders have an alcolock fitted to their cars. Vehicles fitted with this breathalyser device will not start if the driver has been drinking. Other countries where the alcolock is already in use report that many drivers try – and fail – to cheat by connecting pre-inflated balloons to the

mouthpiece. One tried to train his dog to breathe into
the breathalyser.

Guardian/The Times

Government figures show that the cost of owning a
car fell by 11 per cent in real terms between 1975
and 2005. Rail and bus fares climbed 70 per cent
and 66 per cent respectively.

Observer

Plans to allow British drivers to use bus lanes as long as
they carry at least one adult passenger were published
in *The Times* along with details of how drivers in other
countries have tried to cheat:

- By putting life-size inflatable mannequins in
  the passenger seat.
- By having dogs dressed in hats.
- By carrying a stuffed monkey.
- By cruising bus queues touting for
  passengers.
- Hearse drivers have claimed that the dead
  body should be defined as a passenger.
- A pregnant woman claimed she should count
  as two. (She failed.)

Rebecca Denton, 37, who drove a record 30 miles
against oncoming motorway traffic, told police she
thought all the other drivers were on the wrong

side of the road. Swansea Crown Court judge said the case 'defies belief'.

Daily Mirror

Common signs on vans include 'Driver has no access to cash' and 'No tools left in this vehicle overnight.' But Stephen Foster, of Hersham, Surrey, was struck with surprise and amusement to read on a hearse: 'No bodies are left in this vehicle overnight.'

Daily Telegraph

Idris Francis, of Petersfield, Hampshire, was in a car that was being tailgated by a heavy goods vehicle. She rang the HGV's How's My Driving? number and a gruff voice replied: 'Yeah mate – so move over.'

Daily Telegraph

Tim Manns of Southampton reports a van with a sign reading: 'If courteously driven, please report stolen.'

Daily Telegraph

Dawn Forster, 32, passed her test in Middlesbrough after more than 1,000 driving lessons over nine years.

Sun

Speed bumps installed in the picturesque village of Nottington, Dorset, were not appreciated by the locals. Underneath the official sign saying

'NOTTINGTON – Please drive carefully through the village', someone placed another sign saying: 'Twinned with the Himalayas'.

Daily Mail

Mrs Linda Cox of Nottingham sold her car and wrote to her insurers cancelling the policy. They replied: 'The documentation supplied is unacceptable. Please return your current certificate of insurance within seven days. If we do not hear from you by 17.10.04 we will cancel your policy with us.'

The Times

David Mossman, of Caterham, Surrey, received an insurance leaflet suggesting that he could save £200 on his car insurance. The small print in the leaflet said: 'All price saving comparisons are based on a 44-year-old female living in Darlington, with comprehensive cover, zero No Claims Discount, driving 12,999 miles per year in a 2002 Rover 25 1.4.' Mr Mossman says that if the Darlington lady gets in touch he will pass on the leaflet.

The Times

Strathclyde police pulled up a woman learner driver who had a fully dressed blow-up doll wearing a wig sitting next to her – instead of a fully qualified driver as required by law.

Daily Record

Northumbria police spotted Sarah McCaffery, 23, holding an apple while driving. A patrol car, a helicopter and a spotter plane became involved in gathering evidence for a case that involved ten court hearings and is reported to have cost thousands of pounds. Sarah was fined £60 and ordered to pay £100 costs and the *Newcastle Evening Chronicle* described it as a case about an apple that went pear-shaped.

Newcastle Evening Chronicle and national newspapers.

Hemel Hempstead magistrates gave a police car driver four penalty points after he had been clocked doing 97mph while driving David Coleman, the chief constable of Derbyshire, who is an anti-speeding campaigner.

Daily Mail/Sun

The driver of a speed camera van had a good session clocking over two dozen drivers in Oswestry – then was pulled over by a traffic cop and booked for doing 65mph in a 40mph zone.

Sun

'It's L driving with parents' – *Sun* headline on a report saying that some 900,000 young L-drivers have crashed while being taught by their parents. A survey by Direct Line insurance said 31 per cent blamed mum or dad for setting a bad example – with road rage, speeding and tailgating the worst faults.

A speed camera in Nottinghamshire netted more than £4m in fines in five years.

The Times

The Times reported at item broadcast on Radio 4 which identified a road which was to be the subject of a traffic census: 'This will cause delays and drivers are advised to avoid the census point.'

In a typical city centre almost a third of the traffic consists of people driving around looking for somewhere to park.

Independent

Chapter 5

Law and Disorder

**Court allows woman 485 years to pay
back £29,000 debts...**

A collection of bizarre courtroom exchanges in the
Daily Mail included:

Q. Doctor, before you performed the post mortem
    did you feel for a pulse?

A: No

Q: Did you check for breathing?

A: No

Q: So, is it possible that the patient was still alive?

A: No

Q: How can you be so sure?

A: Because his brain was sitting on my desk in a jar.

Two Bradford insurance brokers failed in a court bid to stop their neighbour pretending to have sex with a blow-up sheep. The judge took the view that the man's regular shows at his window did not breach a court order banning him from harassing.

Independent on Sunday

A man I arrested couldn't understand how I knew he was a housebreaker. He was wearing my clothes. Joe Walter, a former Midlands police officer.

Daily Mail

Passage from a solicitor's letter: 'We apologise for the typical graphical error in our previous correspondence'.

Paul McGrath, London EC4, *The Times*

Chesterfield police are seeking two men who have taken to breaking into garden sheds – and tidying them up.

Daily Telegraph

During my first week of duty in the Metropolitan Police in the 1950s I handed in a sixpenny piece found in the street. 'Well done, lad,' said my sergeant. 'Perhaps you could tie a property label on it. I'm a bit busy just now.' Geoffrey Bourne-Taylor, St Edmund Hall, Oxford.

The Times

Margaret Porter, 50, was given a six-year Anti-Social Behaviour Order at Northallerton in North Yorkshire after throwing three sticks of rhubarb at her brother William, 72. Margaret, a farmer's daughter who has won prizes for her giant rhubarb, said: 'My brother was lucky he wasn't hit with one of my prize marrows.'

Sun

A judge dismissed an attempt by Nestle to register the shape of a Polo mint. The food company was appealing against a High Court ruling that it could not trademark the circular shape of the sweet without the word 'Polo' embossed on it. Appeal court judge Lord Justice Mummery said: 'This is an appeal concerning the mint with a hole in the middle. This is an appeal with a hole in the middle. It is dismissed.'

Financial Times

An Englishman's right to fall asleep during a boring football match was solemnly upheld by a court. Judge Michael Taylor dismissed the conviction of Adrian Carr, 28, on a charge of being drunk in a sporting arena during a 4–0 thrashing of Middlesbrough FC by Arsenal. The judge, a Middlesbrough season ticket holder, said: 'It is the right of every Englishman at a football match to fall asleep if he wants, particularly if he's watching Arsenal.'

Guardian/Daily Telegraph

Tony Watson had five saucy gnomes in his garden at Barnsley, South Yorkshire – until police turned up and told him to paint over the naughty bits.

Sun

Police in Guildford are looking for a 'toilet terrorist' who has stolen a master key which he uses to lock people in the Surrey town's public lavatories.

Sun

Shopkeepers burst into laughter when bungling thief Simon Kent, 24, tried to hold them up wearing a plastic bag on his head and carrier bags on his feet. A petrol station attendant told him: 'Bugger off. You look silly.' An off-licence cashier thwarted him by locking herself in a cupboard. Another shop assistant just said 'No' when he demanded cash. Two assistants in a self-service store ran away and he couldn't open the till. Kent's get-away driver did not help by using his own car. Witnesses jotted down his licence number. They both got five years at Lewes Crown Court in Sussex.

Daily Telegraph

Police in Bournemouth aim to cut down on drunken violence by giving chocolate to potential yobs. Thousands of late-night clubbers have been met not by police officers armed with truncheons and CS gas spray, but with packets of Kit Kat Kubes. The scheme is based

on the theory that chocolate induces a general feeling of happiness and reduced aggression.

The Times

Correspondence in the *Daily Mail* tells of some of the games British bobbies play while going about their duties:

- 'The New Year Honours List' – who can make the quickest arrest of the new year.
- 'Trivial Pursuits' – who can get the most ridiculously trivial charge of the month.
- 'The Rainbow' – where cars are stopped in the rainbow's colour order.
- 'Car Snooker' – officers must shop cars in the colours of snooker balls.

A reader told *The Times* how, as a boy, he used to augment his pocket money by pressing Button B in telephone boxes. This was followed by a Kings Lynn reader who said he used to stuff the coin-return chute with cotton wool – and empty it once a week. A third phone box raider recalled that on his way home from church on Sunday mornings he frequently yielded a rich Button B harvest – 'especially from boxes adjacent to pubs.'

A modern version came from a Birmingham man who wrote that, although telephone boxes may no longer have a Button B, he is still unable to pass them without checking the return coin slots. He also checks out car parking machines and reports: 'My local Post Office claims I have been the main prop of its charity coin bottle for several decades.'

The Times

A DIY blunderer who tried to convert his attic into a bedroom made such a hash of it that he risked collapsing his house and the property next door. He caused £15,000 worth of damage and in Leicester Crown Court admitted causing criminal damage. (Sentencing was deferred.)

Daily Telegraph

In 1972, when Sir Robert Mark became Commissioner of the Metropolitan Police, there were reports of police officers taking bribes and fabricating evidence. In his inaugural address Sir Robert reminded his men: 'A good police force is one that catches more criminals than it employs.'

Daily Telegraph

Some saucy garden gnomes who were 'mooning, peeing and taking part in all sorts of activities' were stolen from a garden in Morecambe. The *Lancashire Guardian* headlined the story: 'Dirty Dozen Go AWOL'.

Press Gazette

Superintendent Peter West's home was burgled while he was giving a talk on crime prevention to homeowners in Tenterden, Kent. He said later: 'I have taken further security steps to protect my house.'

Sunday Times

When Jeffrey Archer was in North Sea Camp open prison in Lincolnshire, he met a prisoner who was a genius at making duplicate keys. 'Mick the Key' had used his skills to escape several times from closed prisons. But he gave up making duplicate escape keys after being transferred to North Sea Camp because 'it wouldn't do my reputation any good to escape from an open prison.'

From Archer's *A Prison Diary*
Volume Three in the *Daily Mail*

A Scottish mugger proved easy to track down. He was wearing a Glasgow Rangers shirt with his own name on the back.

Independent on Sunday

A prisoner in Albany Jail on the Isle of Wight was punished for having more than one budgie in his cell. *The Times* revealed just what prisoners are allowed to have in their cells. They include:

- One budgie or canary
- Pictures of Page 3 girls (unless staff object)
- Box of tea bags

- Teddy bear (after being searched for drugs or other contraband)
- Continental quilt

A woman office administrator admitted stealing from the small family business she worked for in Darlington. A county court judge ordered her to pay back £29,246 – at the rate of £5 a month which means she will have 485 years to make up for her dishonesty.

Daily Mail

Yeovil magistrates were told that a local vagrant made around £30,000 a year through aggressive begging and claiming benefits. He was fined £20 and said he would have to go out and beg again to pay the fine.

Guardian/Daily Mail

A hooded 12-year-old boy armed with a double-barrelled sawn-off shotgun held up a shopkeeper in West Bromwich and demanded money and cigarettes. The shopkeeper told him: 'You are not old enough for cigarettes. It is against the law.' He offered the boy sweets instead.

Daily Mirror

Ninety-nine per cent of lawyers give the rest a bad name.
Comedian Steven Wright in *Reader's Digest*

Armed robbers raided a warehouse near Coventry but fled empty handed. They had filled bags so full of coins that they couldn't lift them.

Daily Mirror

Sun columnist Richard Littlejohn keeps track of police activities that might qualify for his *Mind How You Go Awards*. In August 2004 he considered the merits of the following:

- A gay cop is suing Hertfordshire police because he is not allowed to wear his earrings on duty.
- A driving inspector from Blackburn drove through a puddle and splashed a copper standing on the pavement. Although the driver apologised he was taken to court at a cost of £20,000. Magistrates threw out the case.
- Scotland Yard employed a convicted burglar as a policeman for three years.
- Seven officers hid in the bushes in Blackheath, South London, hoping to catch motorists making an illegal left turn.

But Littlejohn's August award went to 'two coppers on crowd control duty in Soho who were discovered having sex in the back of a van with two porn stars.'

Sun

I have received a letter from a solicitor telling me that 'owing to a misunderstanding, my client has not committed adultery'.

P. J. Druce, Witney, Oxfordshire, *The Times*

My solicitor father dictated a letter including the sentence: 'We note you wish to take this matter up again.' When presented for signature, it read: 'We note you wish to rake this matter up again.'

Penelope Gaine, Saffron Walden, Essex, *The Times*

During 35 years in the law I dictated a letter saying that my client had flu. This emerged as: 'My client has fled'.

Bill Knight, London N5 *The Times*

The Prison Service is investigating reports that two inmates sneaked out of Springhill Open Prison in Buckinghamshire, burgled local homes and then returned to jail. Victims included a prison officer. The jailbreakers were caught only when other inmates grassed on them.

Sun

A London police officer works long hours for two months then takes two months off to be with his family – in Dunedin, New Zealand.

Independent

Dorset police sent known criminals picture postcards of prisons along with the message: 'If you don't want to end up here – stop offending.' Police say the cards will show criminals that their cards are marked, but the Howard League for Prison Reform said: 'Most prisoners would just laugh.'

Daily Telegraph/Sun

Two police officers on horseback chased a stolen car through the streets of Middlesbrough. Sparks flew from the horses' hooves as they pounded through the town at full gallop. Two men were arrested after abandoning the car and PC Mark Humble said: 'The chase lasted 20 minutes and I'm sure the horses would have gone on longer.'

Middlesbrough Evening Gazette/Sunday Times

A burglar's getaway was foiled when his false leg fell off as he struggled with the owners of the house he was raiding in Marlow, Buckinghamshire.

Maidenhead Advertiser

A brothel called Temptations in Plymouth was praised by a judge in Truro Crown Court. He said Temptations had treated its prostitutes so well that many had stayed with the company for years. 'If you are going to run a brothel, you could do it a lot worse than this,' he said.

The Times

YOU ABSOLUTELY COULDN'T MAKE IT UP

When mowers belonging to Christopher Robinson of Saffron Walden, Essex, were stolen from an outbuilding, the police seemed fairly uninterested in finding the thief, but inquired if he needed counselling over his sad loss.

The Times

A Dorset man was jailed for robbery after leaving at the scene of the crime – a mobile phone containing a photograph of himself.

Independent on Sunday

Bungling burglar Gary Rickard, 34, was jailed at Exeter Crown Court after being caught having a bath in the house he was raiding. When police came to the bathroom door he shouted: 'Don't come in, I'm having a bath.' The court heard that Rickard had a history of botched break-ins. He was once caught raiding a shop while on crutches with a broken leg.

Daily Mirror/Daily Mail

Southend police drew up a list of time-wasting 999 calls. They included:

- Man complaining that he couldn't sleep because of noisy sex next door.
- Caller wanted action because shop would not give a refund on a fatty sandwich.

- Another dialled the emergency number wanting police to track down a cat that had ripped open bin bags. *Sun*

A management team was sent to Holloway Jail to crack down on its 'sick note culture'. It discovered that one prison officer was on sick leave for more than a year and provided sick notes from a GP – despite having emigrated to New Zealand.

Evening Standard

A century ago the possession and carrying of firearms was perfectly normal in Britain. Guns were sold without licence in ironmongers and department stores such as Selfridges. In 1909 two armed Latvian anarchists attempted to escape by hi-jacking a London tram. They were chased by an extraordinary posse involving police and civilians using horses and carts, cars and bicycles – with some of the locals banging off their own weapons. Before being brought to bay, the fleeing anarchists fired some 400 shots, leaving a policeman and a child dead, and some two dozen other casualties. Policemen in the pursuit borrowed pistols from the civilians because their own weaponry was locked in a gun cupboard and the keys had been mislaid.

Richard Munday, *Sunday Telegraph*

The father of 16-month-old Elliott Nightingale was fined £50 after the baby threw an empty drinks can out of his pram in Oldham. Sixth former Oliver

Thomas, 18, was fined £50 after a slice of tomato fell out of his sandwich in Leeds.

Sun

A teenage couple were banned from speaking to each other for four years under an Anti-Social Behaviour Order imposed by Plymouth Crown Court. The 15-year-olds were accused of terrorising neighbours.

The Times

A 36-year-old man was banned from every garage in Redcar, Cleveland and Middlesbrough under an Anti-Social Behaviour Order imposed by Teeside magistrates. He was accused of cutting fuel lines on pumps and drinking petrol because it gave him a high.

Sun

An Anti-Social Behaviour Order has banned Karen Bulmer, 37, from taking her clothes off in public. She had a habit of doing this after having had a drink and the order was imposed after she stripped off in a police van in York.

Sun

Two brothers annoyed residents in Newton Heath by kicking a football against garage doors. An ASBO banned Liam, 18, and Callum Duff, 17, from playing football in every street in the country.

Sun

Thirteen-year-old Amy Hodges, of Ham Street, near Ashford, Kent, spent four hours in a cell, had her fingerprints taken, was obliged to give a DNA sample, pose for a mugshot and given a formal reprimand – after she threw a snowball which damaged the car of an off-duty special constable. After the off-duty special called in the incident two police cars carrying three officers turned up. Amy said the snowball was thrown during a snowball fight with friends. Kent police said: 'This might be a nice girl from a fine upstanding family – but she broke the law.'

Guardian/Daily Mail

On his way to Ipswich Crown Court to be sentenced for an offence relating to his bankruptcy, Aftab Ahmed, 44, of Bury St Edmunds, Suffolk, got stuck in a traffic jam. While sitting stationary in his car Aftab spoke to Judge Caroline Ludlow on his mobile and she passed sentence on him there and then: 140 hours community punishment and £750 costs. It is believed the phone call made legal history.

Guardian

Gwent police has logged these 'emergency' 999 calls:

- There are rabbits on my lawn – can you move them?
- Is it safe to cook a chicken in the oven overnight?
- There is a dog panting under a tree – it looks as if it needs water. *Independent on Sunday*

Amidst the confusion over the rights of householders to tackle burglars it seems it might be OK to shoot one found still inside the house, but not if he has run outside. Eric Grounds, of Cornhill on Tweed, Northumberland, put this dilemma to his father, then living in California. 'Son,' the father replied, 'you shoot him and then drag him back inside.'

Daily Telegraph

Some years ago, when the Bulmers lived in a remote country house they kept a licensed gun under the bed. Mrs Bulmer asked a crime prevention officer if she could shoot someone entering her bedroom. 'Yes, Madam. Don't miss with the first barrel and put the second into the ceiling to show that you warned him.' Esmond Bulmer, Ripon, North Yorkshire.

Daily Telegraph

Judge Richard Williams gave permission to 999 operators to ignore a woman from Neath, South Wales, who has harassed them with 778 calls costing several thousand pounds. She once dialled because she could not tune her TV.

The Times

Metropolitan policemen 'lost' 1,600 radios over a three-year period. The *Independent* reported that 'scandalously, it seems coppers have been pinching them.' But a Met spokesman said: 'There was a perception that radios were personal-issue and they've been taken inadvertently. We held an amnesty in the summer and eight were handed in.'

Independent

The Hodges family caught a dozy burglar who nodded off while playing games on their inter-active TV in Howey, Mid-Wales.

Sun

They were tough on crime down at the betting office in Tower Hamlets, East London, when a balaclava-clad man burst in screaming: 'I want the money or I will effing shoot you'. The 'gun' the bandit was wielding was inside a bag. But the bag was made from clear plastic and the 'gun' was yellow and sort of bendy. The desperado fled from the shop after staff refused to hand over any money and one of them said: 'I think what this guy has got is actually a banana.' Later a police dog sniffed out the abandoned banana, badly bruised and Southwark Crown Court sent Robert Downey, a previous offender, to jail for six years.

Guardian/Daily Telegraph

A burglar broke into a café on Swindon railway station, drank several cans of lager and then got stuck trying to escape through a window. He had to call for police help and was later fined £420.

The Times

David Harris, 23, pleaded guilty at Guildford Crown Court to possession of cannabis with intent to supply and was given an 18-month community punishment and rehabilitation order. Judge Paul Clements said he was prepared to give Harris the benefit of the doubt after he promised to reform. 'It's a difficult decision,' he said, and added, after a pause: 'All right. It's Friday and the sun is shining... You won't go to prison.'

Daily Telegraph

Angela Wright saw the Freedom of Information Act as a potential way of advancing her private passion – eligible bachelors in uniform. She emailed Hampshire police HQ asking to be told of eligible bachelors between 35 and 49 within the constabulary. Perhaps to her surprise the police replied that they had 266 eligible bachelors with

201 of them being in uniform. But they refused to divulge names and addresses.

Guardian

A couple of students from Cornwall plan to visit America and break as many crazy US laws as possible. They look forward to riding a bike in a swimming pool in Los Angeles, playing cards against a native American in Arizona, whaling in landlocked Salt Lake City, sleeping in a cheese factory in South Dakota, driving non-stop more than 100 times round the town square in Oxford, Mississippi, playing golf in the streets of Albany, New York, using the phrase 'Oh Boy!' in Jonesboro, Georgia, and crossing the road walking on their hands in Hartford, Connecticut.

Guardian

Stephen Winstone, 38, escaped jail because of a grammatical blunder. A court in Weymouth found that it could not convict Winstone of breaching his Anti-Social Behaviour Order because the ASBO stated that he was prohibited from NOT being drunk in public.

The Times

British customs, *see* page 14.

Chapter 6

Wedded Bliss

**Divorce parties arranged with blow-up
toy boys provided...**

In the first year of our marriage I sent my husband a
Valentine. He spent all day trying to guess who had sent
it. In 45 years I have never sent him another.

Elizabeth Ditton, Suffolk, *The Times*

At a wedding reception in Bramhall, Cheshire, the
bride, 39, and groom, 23, started arguing. She hit
him over the head with an ashtray. He threw a hat
stand, javelin-style. Police were called and the
groom butted an officer. He was arrested and
charged with GBH and she went home, cancelled
the honeymoon and filed for divorce.

Independent on Sunday

Referring to a device that prevents drivers exceeding the speed limit, Richard Fuller, of Salisbury, wrote: 'I have one. We have been married for 24 years.'

The Times

Arthur Field of Chichester was pleased with the lovely blouse he bought for his wife at an Oxfam shop where both of them are volunteers. He was proud of knowing her size and the style she liked. 'Yes dear,' said Mrs Field, 'but I donated it to Oxfam yesterday'.

The Times

After it was reported that scientists had produced a vaccine to prevent sheep from breaking wind, Lola Davies, of Firle, East Sussex, wrote to the *Daily Telegraph* saying: 'This makes one feel hopeful that a similar vaccine might become available to owners of Labrador dogs.'

'I am sure there are many wives who would be grateful for the benefits of a wind vaccine in the marital home,' replied P.A. Burbridge from Neston in Cheshire.

In *The Times*' Questions Answered column a reader asks if anything had ever been achieved by putting a message in a bottle and throwing it into the sea. 'Yes', replied Annie Elffers, of Wymondham, Norfolk. 'I did that halfway across the Channel when ten-years-old.

The bottle was found on a Netherlands' beach by a ten-year-old Dutch boy. We have been happily married for nearly 27 years.' When *The Times* interviewed the happy couple, Mrs Elffers told how she first met the boy when she was 12, during a family holiday in the Netherlands. 'I particularly liked the way he did cartwheels down the street,' she said.

Lily Tang Yu and Morgan O'Hara were born within a few miles of each other at exactly 6.20pm on 8 August 1974. They went to the same school in Rochdale and became sixth form sweethearts. They married in April 2004 in the local church. It has been estimated that the chances of all this happening are 4.3million to one.

Daily Mirror

It is a happy reflection of our longer lives that card manufacturers print 100th birthday cards. American friends expressed surprise that – in the UK at least – manufacturers still consider golden wedding cards a viable proposition.

Jan Snook, Bramley, Surrey, *The Times*

My local post office had no Golden Wedding cards, but five different 'Congratulations on your Divorce' cards.

John Burscough, Hibaldstow, Brigg, *The Times*

Despite bearing the headline 'Cuddles, Snuggles and Cootchy-Cootchy-Pumpkin', a *Times* leader on

Valentine's Day reminded readers of a survey which claimed that partnerships are five times more likely to break up on 14 February than any other day. Also St Valentine himself was probably celibate.

The Times

Criminal gangs are beating immigration rules by setting up bogus marriages. *The Times* reported some of the tell-tale signs which rouse suspicion:

- **The bride screws up her face when kissed by the groom.**
- **The groom tries to kiss the witness.**
- **Bride and groom need interpreters to speak to each other.**
- **The groom demands the ring back after the ceremony.**

An industry has grown up to help people celebrate their divorces. One event-management company advertises its divorce party amenities alongside its arrangements for wedding and birthday celebrations. A director of the company said most divorce parties were held by women and 'lots of alcohol is consumed with dancing and general bitching about men.' One of the parties had handsome young men in tiny shorts serving canapés and drinks. Another company sells divorce party accessories which include an inflatable toy boy in a tin.

The Times

Chapter 7

Not Dead,
Just Resting

Theatre wants dead actor to play dead actor...

*I*n an article in *The Times* Alan Coren asked: 'On the day you die, what do you want people to say about you?' My sister's reply: 'She made good gravy.'

Molly Craven, Brighton.

Keith Waterhouse's oldest friend Willis Hall died in March 2005. They had been partners in stage and screen collaborations for more than 40 years and Keith's mind flew back to the death of another old friend. A woman said then: 'Oh dear, was he poorly?' 'If he wasn't, luv,' said Willis, 'we've just buried the wrong bloke.'

Daily Mail

Jacqueline Loxton, of Bradford-on-Avon, Wiltshire, tells of the days her husband held the post of Director of Physical Training and Sport for the Royal Navy. On his desk was a sign reading: 'I get all the exercise I need by acting as pall bearer to my more athletic friends.'

Daily Telegraph

'It is sad to learn that Spike Milligan's grave has still not got a headstone,' wrote James Wild, a member of the Spike Milligan Memorial Campaign, which is dedicated to remembering the legendary Goon with a statue in Lewisham High Street. 'So take heart, and remember his quote about heaven: 'I'd like to go there. But if Jeffrey Archer is there I want to go to Lewisham.'

Independent

Spike Milligan's desire to have 'I told you I was sick' on his headstone, prompted M.J.F. Wardroper, of Berwick, East Sussex, to remember one he saw for a philandering husband which reads: 'At least I know where he is sleeping tonight'.

Daily Telegraph

At Rochdale cemetery there is a sign which reads: 'Exit and Way Out'.

Spotted by R. Taylor of Rochdale, Lancs, *Daily Mail*

Ad in Classic Car Mart: 'Ford Granada Hearse. 90,000 miles. Superb engine and gearbox. Body in good condition.'

Daily Telegraph

A bank manager my wife worked for dictated a letter concerning the death of a customer who had died intestate. It came back from the typing pool as 'died in Tescos'.

Alan Saunders, Exeter, *The Times*

The Rev. W.N.C. Girard, of Balsham, Cambridge-shire wrote to the *Daily Telegraph* about a lawyer's bill sent to the estate of a man whose will he had drawn up. It included the item: 'To attending on you for your signature, but you were dead.'

The 11th Duke of Devonshire died in May 2004. Long obituaries in all the papers included:

- **When miners launched a protest meeting outside his stately home, Chatsworth, in Derbyshire, the Duke met them on a cold morning carrying a large silver tureen of hot consommé laced with sherry.**
- **The wife of miners' leader Arthur Scargill said: 'Such a gent. We couldn't get cross with him.'**
- **When asked if he belonged to the elite**

establishment club Pratt's, he replied: 'In fact, it belongs to me.'

- 'My entire life has been a battle against indolence. I have achieved absolutely nothing. It's quite shaming.'
- When his uncle, Harold Macmillan, became prime minister, he brought the Duke into his government and the Duke later said it was 'the single worst act of nepotism'.
- When age slowed him down the Duke said: 'The days of fast women and slow horses are behind me.'
- He was an English gentleman. The aristocrats' aristocrat.' From *The Times*, *Daily Telegraph*, *Guardian* and *Daily Mail*

Burnley Council wants funeral directors to hold the cremations of fat people only in the mornings. It says that anyone weighing more than 19 stones should not be cremated much later than 9.30am because their ashes clog up the burners.

Sunday Telegraph

Thieves who stole a hearse in Bury, Greater Manchester, abandoned it in a street nearby. It had a body in the back.

Guardian

Ashes to ashes. Marie Ellis, a lifelong smoker, died aged 105 and was cremated clutching a packet of her favourite Benson & Hedges. She had puffed 15 a day since she was 15, smoking a total of nearly half a million cigarettes. Marie was sent off with a rousing chorus of Smoke Gets in Your Eyes and her main wreath was in the shape of a cork-tipped cigarette. The old people's home where she lived in Westgate, Kent, plan a concrete, ashtray-shaped memorial for her.

Daily Telegraph/Sun

Marie's cremation inspired the *Sun* to dig up some other wacky funerals, including:

- Dr Who fan Tim Haws, 43, buried in a Tardis in Hurstpierpoint, West Sussex.
- Tony Goldsworthy, 70, had his ashes shot skywards by fellow members of the Bath Muzzle and Historic Breechloaders Association.
- Alan Smith, 65, of Cornwall, had his remains loaded onto a Viking longboat which was set alight at sea.
- Green Party leader Mike Woodin, 38, stuck to his principles and was buried in a biodegradable cardboard box towed to Oxford cemetery by a bicycle.
- East End pub landlord Cyric, 58, was buried

with a floral tribute in the shape of a bottle of brandy.

An experimental London theatre group known as 1157 planned a production involving 'a serious examination of the taboos surrounding death'. It announced a casting call with a difference – aspiring actors had to agree to be dead by the time the show opened.

Observer/The Age (Australia)

The late Ronnie Bellamy, 84, of Barnstaple, Devon, had details of his funeral printed on pub beer mats for the benefit of his drinking pals.

Sun

Times readers responded to an invitation to reveal what music they would choose for their funerals. Among the choices were:

- *Smoke Gets in Your Eyes* (for a cremation)
- *Knocking on Heaven's Door* (to signify hope over expectation)
- *Please Don't Talk About Me When I'm Gone*
- *Sheep May Safely Graze* (for a Berkshire butcher)

Ave Maria and Mozart's *Requiem* are favourites at funerals in France, Spain and Italy, but among the top ten in Britain are Robbie Williams' 'Angels', Frank Sinatra's 'My Way', Monty Python's 'Always Look on the Bright Side of Life' and Queen performing 'Who Wants to Live Forever'.

Daily Telegraph/Times/Sun

Parachute for sale, *see* page 17.

Chapter 8

Just Lie Back and Think of England

She only swears when it slips out...

Question: Who first lay back and thought of England?
Answer from N.G. Macbeth of Kenilworth: Alice, Lady
Hillingdon, in her journal, 1912: 'I am happy now that
Charles calls on my bedchamber less frequently. I now
endure but two calls a week. I lie down on my bed, close
my eyes, open my legs and think of England.'

Guardian

A retired Welsh miner claimed that he had slept with
200 women he met through an Internet dating agency.
His name was removed from the database after
women complained that he lacked commitment.

Daily Express/Sunday Telegraph

Any suggestions for a suitable twinning partner for Intercourse, Pennsylvania?

Joseph Cocker, Leominster, Hereford. *Guardian*

Condom, in France.

John Hannavy, Standish, Lancashire, *Guardian*

Intercourse could do worse than choose the neighbouring town of Paradise. For those who live in the north-eastern part of Pennsylvania the route to Paradise is through Intercourse.

Mike Mann, Bedford, *Guardian*

Having seen a touring production of Hamlet, a college professor asked the director whether he believed the Prince of Denmark had actually consummated his relationship with Ophelia.

'Yes,' replied the director. 'I think it was during the second week at the Grand Theatre, Wolverhampton.'

Daily Telegraph

The version of the Hamlet/Ophelia joke as I heard it in the 1950s concerned an actor interviewed in old age: 'In your view, sir, does Hamlet go to bed with Ophelia?'

'Almost invariably.'

Sir Tom Stoppard, London SW10,
Daily Telegraph

The version I heard gave the punchline to John Barrymore. A drama student asked him: 'Do you think Hamlet and Ophelia ever slept together?'

Barrymore replied in a whisper: 'Only in the Chicago company.' Herbert Kretzmer, London W8.

Daily Telegraph

A sex survey claims that an orgasm burns off 27 calories, but faking it uses 160.

Sun

A report in the *New Scientist* saying that around one in ten have no interest in bonking inspired a Sunday broadsheet newspaper to produce an A–Z of sex. It included:

- Foreplay ('the petting before the getting') varies enormously. In Thailand lovers scarcely bother. Unbelievably, the British come top with 22.5 minutes.
- Uxorobolent – a condition in which a man can achieve fulfilment only when having intercourse with his wife.
- Uxoravalent – when a man gets fulfilment only extramaritally.
- Zoophiles. People who have sex with animals. A man from Hull was jailed for six months after being caught in an uncompromising position with a goat on

a crowded train. He said it was 'a spontaneous act.'

Observer

Donald McGill's saucy postcards became a traditional part of British seaside holidays and their double entendres are now regarded as a bit of innocent fun. But half a century ago they shocked local council 'watch committees' into banning them and he was once dragged into court and fined. The *Guardian* reports that one 'apparently innocuous card' was banned, with stocks being destroyed, in 20 towns. It featured a smartly dressed girl walking past two men who remark: 'She's a nice girl. Doesn't drink or smoke and only swears when it slips out.' The second most complained-of card showed two little girls bathing a baby boy, with one of them commenting: 'It isn't a whistle, I tried.'

If governments were really serious about taxing youth they would tax sex. Unfortunately, apart from the practical problem of assessing liability, this would likely accelerate population decline. If humans are to go on reproducing, the young need all the practice they can get.

Financial Times leader

Many young people believe that closing their eyes while having sex will guard against pregnancy. Others think that standing on telephone directories, drinking milk or jumping up and down afterwards will do the trick.

Daily Telegraph on a report in
Doctor magazine

The *Doctor* magazine was reporting on a survey that asked British doctors to list the old wives' tales about pregnancy cited by their young patients. It revealed that making love in a boat or in the bath, or drinking rum and coke are also regarded by some as reliable contraception.

There's a website offering to supply naked butlers for hen nights – www.butlersinthebuff.com

Sunday Times

Single Britons are the most promiscuous in the world. An international survey found that 59 per cent of Britons thought it normal for a thirty-something to have had ten or more lovers before getting married. In China the figure was 17 per cent, France 30 per cent, US 49 per cent, Germany 52 per cent.

Guardian

Since mobile phones became so popular 40,000 of Britain's 72,000 street public telephone boxes make a loss and a *Daily Telegraph* writer asked: When did you last see anybody using one? A reader pointed out that the most important use for the telephone box these days is for adulterous liaison. Because there are detailed records available of calls from other phones 'no self-respecting philanderer would ever use anything other than an untraceable call from a phone box. Long may they remain.' Chris Doe of London N1 wrote in to say that telephone boxes provide shelter for using mobiles when it is raining.

Daily Telegraph

It's 40 years old now – and when the *Sunday Times* reproduced some of the Pirelli calendar's sexy shots down the years it asked the question: 'Is it a porn fest for motor executives or a pictorial comment upon the times?' It also revealed that you won't be able to buy the glossy calendar in the shops, nor will you be able to send off for one. Only 400 copies are printed for the UK and, of those, one goes to the Prime Minister and six go to Buckingham Palace.

Allan MacCarthy of London SE7 was surprised to find in a well-known bookshop… sex manuals on the DIY shelf.

Observer

East Midlands men paying £1 a minute to talk to Filipino girls on a sex line complained when the so-called exotic females used phrases such as 'Ey up' and 'Cheers me duck'. Nottingham magistrates fined the man who ran the line £65 with £1,000 costs for describing 40 local girls as Filipinas.

The Times

Deodorant instructions, *see* page 17.

Chapter 9

Animal Magic

Website finds lovers for lonely pets...

Mrs M. McCulloch, of Leeds, caught her grandson brushing the dog's teeth with his toothbrush. She told him it was a filthy habit and he replied: 'I usually use yours, but I couldn't find it today.'

Daily Mail

The sounds of laughter echoed across the Henley Rotary Club's lunch when the speaker, retired vet David Williamson, spoke of his early life as a vet in a cowshed. He told of the chap who lit a match to check the gas coming out of the rear end of a cow and burnt down the farm.

Henley Standard

When Luton magistrates banned Jackie Jefferson, 41, from keeping animals she told the court: 'I've got a goldfish.' The advice that came down from the bench was: 'Eat it'.

Sun

Seagulls at Sidmouth have been attacking men with bald heads. Locals fight them off with high-powered water pistols.

Daily Telegraph

Staff at Battersea Dogs Home were baffled when, night after night, a group of dogs escaped from their bolted pens and went for midnight feasts in the kitchen. Surveillance cameras were installed and they revealed that Red, a lurcher now called Houdini, had learned how to unbolt his pen with his teeth. He then went round freeing around nine of his mates to join the party. Battersea staffer Liz Emery said: 'They had lots of food, lots of fun and caused lots of mess.'

Independent, The Times, Sun, Daily Telegraph, Evening Standard, Daily Mail and practically every other paper in the land

A posse of 20 pet lovers in Jesmond, Newcastle-upon-Tyne, rushed to the aid of a goldfish trapped in a roadside drain. They included two council workmen, five railway workers, staff from a nearby pub and an RSPCA inspector. All their efforts failed until 13-year-old Nishtaj Misra ran home and brought back a fishing net. The goldfish looked very dead when it was pulled from the drain, but then it suddenly moved.

'Everyone cheered,' said Nishtaj. 'It was lovely.'

Daily Telegraph

In the village of Yarlington, Somerset, they indulge in a game called Cowpat Roulette. A field is divided into small squares which are 'sold' for £1 each. Cows are then released into the field and the first one to perform on a square wins a prize for the square's 'owner'. Geoffrey Self, Ilminster, Somerset.

Daily Telegraph

A three-week-old kitten called Kitty got stuck in a drainpipe under the kitchen of its owner, Denise Machin of Bristol. A 999 call brought two fire engines and the RSPCA to the scene. Firemen with a mechanical hammer (normally used to free people from car wrecks) failed to get close to Kitty. After two hours of chipping away at pipes and brickwork they sucked the kitten to freedom with the family's Dyson vacuum cleaner.

Daily Mail

Celia Haddon is the *Daily Telegraph's* pet agony aunt and author of many books on cats. Her husband Ronnie Payne has written a book entitled *100 Ways To Live With*

A Cat Addict. Here are three gems from the book:

- Whenever your partner says in a special soft voice: 'Darling, come here. I really love you!' he or she is almost certainly addressing the cat. Learn to live with this.
- A well-directed puff of old shag pipe tobacco is enough to put the boldest tom to flight.
- Feline fascination with what the humans are up to must have spoiled more nights of passion than grey flannel knickers ever did. Keep cats out of the bedroom.

The *Daily Telegraph* had a letter saying cycling game wardens in African safari parks are called Meals on Wheels. Sandra Rice, of Warwick, followed up with a sign in an Australian safari park: 'These animals are dangerous. Do not leave your vehicle. Entrance $5. Poms on bicycles – free'.

Daily Telegraph

Pet owners take eight million 'sickies' a year off work to grieve over the death of their animals.

Daily Mail

A goose picked up a golf ball on a course in Scarborough, Yorkshire and began nesting on it, thinking it was an egg.

Sun

Vets in Manchester had to operate on a German Shepherd dog after it swallowed 28 golf balls.

Sun

Percy — a very cocky peacock — has adopted the Rectory of the Northamptonshire village of Walgrave as his territory. He visits the Royal Oak on the village green every day for his free pub lunch and treats the customers to impressive tail displays. He loves nothing better than an appreciative audience.

Rev. D.G. Thomas, Northamptonshire
Daily Telegraph

As English football fans risked nervous breakdowns urging Sven's team to win, they were warned not to let their dogs view the Euro 2004 clashes. The European Animal and Nature Protection Society said pets can be left emotionally scarred by their owners' angry reactions. Vets advised that dogs should be taken out of the room when matches were on TV.

Daily Telegraph

A black doberman-labrador cross named Jasper has been named one of Britain's most pampered pets. Jasper lives with Sir Benjamin Slade near Bridgwater, Somerset, and dines on medium rare sirloin steak, Dover sole and freshwater mussels. He travels in a stretch limo and has his own portfolio of shares.

Sunday Times

Many owners are taking their pet dogs to special swimming pools where the water is heated and there are changing rooms with powerful hair dryers. Dogs visiting for the first time can hire water wings.

Daily Mail

In a one-hour operation Swansea vets removed four large socks from the stomach of Spud, a cross-bred terrier puppy. Spud ate the socks while his owner Jennie Jones was loading a washing machine.

Sunday Telegraph

Forget James Bond. During the cold war MI5 considered a plan to send squadrons of kamikaze pigeons to dive-bomb the Kremlin carrying tiny biological bombs.

Sun

This worried Sheila Kay, of Lewes, East Sussex, who wrote to the *Guardian* saying: 'I thought pigeons were trained to fly straight home.'

A Glasgow pet foods firm is to introduce designer water for pets to combat bad breath. Mouth-watering flavours, including chicken and parsley-chlorophyll, are to be offered for dogs, cats, birds, hamsters and even snakes and lizards.

Guardian

A deaf German Shepherd puppy is being taught sign language at a dog centre in Bournemouth.

Sun

Spinster Nora Hardwell left £450,000 in her will to provide for the future care of her two collie-cross bitches Tina and Kate. They have the run of her home, set in four acres of lawns and semi-woodland near Peasedown St John, Somerset and are looked after by gardener and maintenance man Henry Escott. Henry received £5,000 in her will.

Daily Telegraph

A couple who between them smoked 50 cigarettes a day gave up the habit for the sake of JJ – their African parrot. Kevin Barclay, 42, of Shoeburyness, Essex, and his partner were told by a vet that JJ was wheezing because of passive smoking.

Daily Telegraph

When a bonfire was lit at Devizes Cricket Club in Wiltshire, a rabbit jumped out with its tail on fire and ran under the groundsman's hut. It caused a fire that damaged £60,000 worth of equipment. Devizes firemen recorded their regret that they had been unable to save the rabbit.

Daily Telegraph

The *Derby Mercury* reported on 28 February 1777 that a ship's cat caught fire when a hot coal fell on its back soon after 'one of the finest vessels in the coastal trade between London and Gainsborough had arrived in the Trent.' The cat ran into a cargo of hemp which began to blaze and the *Mercury* reported: 'As there were twenty barrels of gun powder aboard the crew was obliged to quit the vessel for fear of the consequences. About nine o'clock in the evening she blew up and sunk and all her goods were rolled out by the tide, so that there remains but one puncheon of rum and two or three barrels of porter.'

Like the rabbit, the cat did not survive, writes Janet Spavoid of Ashby de la Zouch in the *Daily Telegraph*.

Over the years, animal lover Jean Pike has buried 22 pets along with her husband Theo at the bottom of her garden on Hayling Island, Hampshire. She makes a daily pilgrimage to their tombstones and has stipulated that she will eventually take her place beside them.

Daily Mirror

A *Daily Telegraph* leader opined that foreigners reading the story of Dino, the German Shepherd who bit a woman, will take it as further evidence that the British are mad. Dino was condemned to death by magistrates but his owners then spent

100

three years and some £60,000 fighting the decision. They did battle in a Northampton Crown Court, the High Court, the House of Lords the European Court of Human Rights and finally the Criminal Cases Review Commission before Dino was reprieved. The *Telegraph* leader rejoiced and said: 'Dino now takes his place in the glorious annals of British justice. We just hope he behaves himself from now on.'

When Judge Patrick Eccles lifted Dino's death sentence he was moved to quote Hamlet: 'Every dog will have his day.'

Guardian

Britain's pampered pet dogs now have their own dating agency. Owners can register them on a lonely hearts website called Cold Nose, Warm Heart, which promises 'a discreet and confidential service.'

Sunday Telegraph/India Daily

Britain is a nation of fat cats, corpulent canines and lardy rabbits. In October 2004 the *Guardian* said that almost 80 per cent of UK vets reported an increase in the number of obese pets they were having to treat. Perhaps pet owners should follow the example reported in an earlier edition of this book (from the *Daily Mail* of 10 December 2002): 'When the Grimson's vet in Ilkley, Yorkshire, said that their fat labrador Henry must diet,

they felt it was only fair that they should join him. Henry lost two stone. Joy Grimson lost three stone. Husband David and son Oliver shed two stone between them.'

They have got it wrong, those macho types who think of Staffordshire bull terriers as vicious brutes that look good at one end of a chain wrapped around a tattooed fist. So much so that many Staffies end up at Battersea Dogs Home because they fail to live up to this image and turn out to be softies who are good with children. When they arrive at the Home they have names such as Rommel, Adolf, Bruiser, Tyson, Storm, Rambo, Thunder and Venom. The Home renames them with more innocuous monikers like Bubbles, Cheeky, Cuddles, Kiss, Lolly, Romeo, Sage, Splodge, Sugar and Sweet Pea.

Daily Telegraph

Six 'gay' male penguins in a German zoo made front-page news in British newspapers when the zoo announced plans to introduce them to some female penguins. The males had been observed trying to mate with each other and trying to hatch stones. The zoo's plans to provide girlfriends sparked outrage among gay and lesbian groups who insisted that the penguins had the right to form couples without human interference.

Daily Telegraph and others

Marilyn King's vet in Cumbernauld, near Glasgow, was baffled when her parrot Nelson developed a racking cough. The 13-year-old bird was wheezing and apparently struggling for breath. Medical tests costing £100 failed to pinpoint the cause of the symptoms. It was then discovered that Nelson had previously lived in an old people's home and was simply mimicking the sounds he had heard there.

Daily Mail

Thanks to the Freedom of Information Act, the *Daily Telegraph* has been rummaging through the official file on Humphrey, the one-time official mouser at 10 Downing Street. Humphrey arrived at the Cabinet Office uninvited as a one-year-old in 1989, following a long line of distinguished government mousers dating from the reign of Henry VIII. In March 1992 an official memo was prepared on Humphrey, revealing that he was costing the taxpayer £100 a year to feed and was rather more effective than a professional pest controller who charged £4,000 a year.

The *Illustrated London News* requested an interview but was told: 'Unfortunately, as a civil servant, Humphrey cannot talk to the press.'

Humphrey's title was Chief Mouser to the Cabinet Office, but when the Blairs arrived at No.10 in May 1997, rumours gripped the nation that the new residents wanted him out. On 12 November 1997 a memo was prepared saying that it was time for ailing Humphrey to retire 'to a stable home environment' and the Downing Street press office prepared a press release breaking the news to the world. His destination was kept secret 'to avoid would-be catnappers'. The *Daily Telegraph* reported in March 2005: 'Where Humphrey is now – or even whether he is still with us – remains a mystery... The cat's abrupt departure six months after Labour won the election took the gloss off Mr Blair's landslide election.'

In the days when the public could wander along Downing Street, two Americans met Humphrey. He sniffed at their lower limbs and then strolled on. Later the Americans told the officer guarding No.10 that they were amazed at the low level of security. 'How do you know we are not armed?' they asked. Adopting a conspiratorial mode, the constable said: 'Remember the cat that sniffed you and then walked on? He is a specially trained Metropolitan cat and can smell firearms and explosives and, should you have had either, would have warned me.'

Chris Walker, *Daily Telegraph*

Sir Bernard Ingham, who was press secretary to Margaret Thatcher when she was prime minister, wrote in to say that the cat involved in Chris Walker's story could not have been Humphrey – but a predecessor called Wilberforce. He remembers Lady Thatcher buying Wilberforce a tin of sardines during a visit to Moscow.

Daily Telegraph

99.9 percent bacteria, *see* page 32.

Chapter 10

Raise Your Glasses

Beer swilling magpie barred from pub...

The bar group Brannigans – fed up with how long women spend in the toilets – plans to try out cubicle doors that spring open 60 seconds after they shut in a scheme to flush out time-wasters.

Daily Mail

A pub chain in the North of England called Yesteryear is to stick strategically placed, realistic-looking transfers of spiders on its men's urinals to encourage 'a far higher standard of accuracy.' It is expected that there will be a far lower level of splashage if gentlemen have something to aim at.

Guardian

A vet in Welshpool, Powys, was puzzled by Trixie – a cat that kept falling over. Then he discovered Trixie lived at a local pub and was addicted to lapping up the drip trays.

Daily Express

A prisoner with a drink problem escaped from Prescoed open prison in South Wales because there was too much illicit drinking going on. When recaptured he was granted his wish to finish his sentence in a tougher prison away from temptation.

Sun/South Wales Argus

In spite of traditional Welsh nonconformist antipathy to strong drink, intoxicating beverages can now be imbibed at the Eisteddfod, Wales's annual cultural festival. Might as well, because BBC Wales used to get around the ban by serving wine in teapots. 'You could hear 'tea' being poured from 11.30am,' said a source.

Daily Mail

To celebrate the British fascination with garden sheds, the Discovery Home & Leisure TV channel holds a Shed of the Year contest. There was no surprise when Darren Hindley of Ripon got into the top ten in 2004. He's built an entire pub inside his shed, complete with bar, dartboard, pewter tankards, barrel seats, fridge, TV and 'Rules of the Inn' pinned to the wall. 'It's every bloke's dream,' he says.

Evening Standard/Ripon News

Lucy Hammond, 72, won a hanging basket contest in Marlborough, Wiltshire, after giving her plants a tipple of vintage port once a week.

Sun

When Bill Clinton visited Northern Ireland during his presidency US security men were horrified to discover that there was a bar called Monica's along his route. To prevent the media using it as an excuse to bring the Lewinsky affair into their reports, they persuaded the owner to change the name for 24 hours and to hang a new sign outside the pub.

The Times

A beer-swilling magpie has been barred from the King's Arms in Heath Common, Wakefield, West Yorkshire. At first regulars were amused when the magpie swooped in to take a swig from their pints, but the novelty wore off and now landlord Alan Tate 'escorts' the flying lager lout from the premises.

Daily Mail

Alan Morgan, 62, asked for a tonic water with ice and lemon when he visited the Empire Club in Rhymney Valley, South Wales. He was stunned when the barmaid said; 'It's not a cocktail bar, you know.' A club official said: 'We have never had a call for lemons. They are not called for in the Valleys. My wife brings her own. Somebody once called for Smirnoff Ice and within a fortnight we got it in.' The issue is to be raised at a meeting of the club committee.

Daily Telegraph

The Welsh slice of lemon story (above) reminded David Ross, of Liverpool, of ordering a glass of dry white wine in the plush cocktail bar of the Philharmonic Dining Rooms in that city in 1971. 'My order was rejected out of hand with the words: "This is not a plonky house."'

Daily Telegraph

Nearly two thirds of British adults believe that the pub has more to offer the community than the church, according to a survey by InnSpired (which owns more than 1,000 pubs). Kate Fox, co-director of the Social Issues Research Centre, said: 'The bar of the pub is one of the very few public places in England where it is socially acceptable to strike up a conversation with a complete stranger.'

The Times

Landlord Aidan Mahon got fed up with his regulars claiming that Guinness tasted better in Ireland than in his Norwich pub. He paid £5,000 to fly 48 of them to Dublin to prove them wrong. Unfortunately the regulars said that the trip proved their point.

Daily Telegraph

The year 2005 opened with controversy raging over proposals to let pubs and clubs open 24 hours a day. Would this lead to an explosion in the increasingly popular British pastime of binge drinking? The *Sun* reminded its readers that British binge-drinking was nothing new in a report headlined: 'The Sobering Truth Behind The Big 24-hour Pubs Debate'. The report pointed out:

- Some historians believe excessive boozing cost us the Battle of Hastings in 1066. Many of King Harold's soldiers failed to turn up because they were hung over from celebrating victory over the Vikings at the Battle of Stamford Bridge three weeks earlier.
- The Duke of Wellington, famous for beating Napoleon in 1815, complained that 'English soldiers are fellows who have all enlisted for a drink.'
- The Normans encouraged the building of monasteries and abbeys, each with a brewery. They supplied travellers out of Christian duty and allowed monks a daily allowance of nine pints of beer – and this was seen as erring on the mean side.
- The Royal Navy used to give sailors eight pints of beer a day. In 1731 this was switched to half a pint of rum.

- Oliver Cromwell and the Puritans clamped down on drinking in the 1650s and drinking became punishable by flogging or a spell in the stocks.
- But when the Royalists returned in 1660 Charles II was known as the Merry Monarch – and binge-drinking became almost the social norm.
- In the 1840s teetotallers had to pay extra for life insurance, because drinking the water available in those days was looked upon as foolhardiness.
- In some parts of London one house in four sold gin either legally or illegally. A sign from those days reads: 'Drunk for one penny. Dead drunk for tuppence.'

In 1830 an Act was introduced allowing anyone to set up a beer-only pub in order to wean people off foreign drink and support the British beer industry. Within weeks 30,000 beer houses opened up. Andrew Davison, co-author of the English Heritage book *Licensed to Sell*, says: 'The country was paralytic for a month and the law was soon repealed.'

Guardian

School's Out

Tap-dancing pupils told to do it quietly...

A list of 20 top clangers in GCSE exam papers, revealed by government education officials, included:

- A myth is a female moth.
- Joan of Arc was burnt to a steak.
- Francis Drake circumcised the world with a 100ft clipper.
- Ancient Egypt was inhabited by mummies who wrote in hydraulics.
- Beethoven wrote loud music because he was deaf.
- Socrates died from an overdose of wedlock.

The Times

British school reports are not as devastating as they used to be. Political correctness and the threat of litigation have forced teachers to tone down their criticism.

In the days when they were 'waspish, witty, frequently cruel and usually wrong,' Winston Churchill's masters found him "weak'" at geography and "not very good" at French'. He was 'troublesome', 'very naughty' and could not 'be trusted to behave himself anywhere'.

Michael Heseltine was 'rebellious, objectionable, inefficient, antagonising, untidy, conceited, impertinent, lazy and smug'.

Jilly Cooper 'set herself an extremely low standard which she failed to maintain'.

John Lennon was 'hopeless... certainly on the road to failure'.

The Times reporting on a collection of school reports entitled *Could Do Better*, edited by Catherine Hurley.

Charles Wilkie-Smith, of Corbridge, Northumberland, recalled his final prep school history report which said: 'Charles Smith slept here.'

The Times

Andy Du Port, of Chichester, West Sussex, was taught rowing and geography by the same master and got a school report that said: 'Good at rivers.'

The Times

An exasperated colleague wrote on one pupil's school report: 'John is to design technology what Attila the Hun was to needlework.' Henry Adams, Wirral.

The Times

In the 1960s I was told that the only words required in school reports were: 'Trying' and 'Very'.

Jean Bryant, East Grinstead, West Sussex,
The Times

Arnold Freedman treasures his school report saying: 'Should have done well, but has fallen into bad company.' In a letter to *The Times* he reports: 'I became a consultant surgeon. The bad company became a professor of physics.'

School report on the son of a professor of mathematics: 'Not up to pa.'

Robert Hudson, Warwick, *The Times*

A report from the Latymer Upper School, Hammersmith, London: 'We have both failed. I, at least, tried.'

Kenneth Cleveland, Carlisle, *The Times*

A head teacher remembers this report: 'I have spent more time on X's homework than he has.'

David Porter, Bury St. Edmunds, Suffolk,
The *Times*

Lee Jones of Manchester got a note from school complaining about 'incomplete and poorly attempted' homework. He admitted that he had not submitted homework for some time, but pointed out that he is now approaching his 21st birthday and left school four years ago.

Sun

DJ John Peel, who died in October 2004, used to tell how, 'bearing in mind that my name is John', his primary school headmistress had reported: 'Robin has failed to make much impression this year.'

The Times

Research by a vacuum-cleaner manufacturer found that the amount of dirt found in students' rooms is more than 30 times that detected on the floor of a typical pub.

Daily Telegraph

At my boys' grammar school back in the mid-1950s, a delegation of boys asked the head if the end-of-term dances with girls from a nearby school could end at midnight instead of 11pm. He replied: 'Gentlemen, if you have not achieved your objectives between 8pm and 11pm it is highly unlikely that you will succeed between 11pm and midnight.'

John Hoben, Falmouth, Cornwall, *The Times*

A meeting of tutors and undergraduates at Liverpool University in the 1960s debated the ban on girls in Rathbone Hall after 11pm. The students' plea that nothing could happen at night between men and women that was not possible during the day was met by an interjection from an elderly tutor, hitherto apparently comatose, exclaiming: 'Ah! But they could do it again!' John Horrocks, University of the West of England.

The Times

In a BBC survey almost half of 16 to 24 year olds could not identify William the Conqueror as the victor of the Battle of Hastings.

- More than one in five believed it was Alexander the Great.
- 13 per cent said it was Napoleon.
  Daily Mail

Pupils are to be encouraged to experiment with oral sex in a bid to cut down on teenage pregnancies.

Observer/Sun

'St Paul's School requires leaning assistant to support class teacher.'

Ad in the *Evening Mail*, Birmingham

Reader's Digest asked a nationally representative sample of teachers what they wished they could say to parents:

- Helping your child with homework doesn't mean letting him lift it off the internet.
- Your daughter has a mobile phone and a CD player in school, so why no pen, pencil or handkerchief?
- Your child's performance in PE is so low because he is so fat.

A survey found four per cent of British children were under the impression that Hitler was prime minister of the UK during World War II. From a book called *Numbers* by David Boyle and Anita Roddick, quoted in the *Daily Mail*.

The John Barras pub chain is providing calculators for its younger darts players. They are so poor at maths that they hold up the game.

Daily Telegraph

Suffolk County Council is advertising for a £500-a-week 'garbologist' to teach schoolchildren about waste disposal.

Daily Telegraph

Children taking tap dancing lessons at Reddings & District Community Centre in Cheltenham have been told to train on soft mats after their dancing was blamed for marking the wooden floor. Organisers of the classes fumed: 'Whoever heard of silent tap dancing?' They are looking for a new venue.

Daily Mail

Michael Sheahan, who teaches English in Paris, asked his students to name the ten most famous Britons. Princess Diana topped the list, David Beckham was fifth, Mr Bean sixth, Elton John seventh, Benny Hill eighth, Shakespeare, ninth. Number ten was a tie between the Queen and Sean Connery.

Guardian

Drunken dentistry, *see* page 37.

Chapter 11

Plain Eccentric

Prince Charles is potty about lavatory seats...

Following newspaper stories about men wearing ladies' tights to keep warm, Stuart Hamilton of Derbyshire wrote to the *Daily Telegraph* about a hunting gentleman who was asked how long he had been wearing such tights. The reply: 'Ever since my wife found a pair in the back of my car.'

A reader from West Byfleet, Surrey, writes about an aunt who always kept a hat in the hall. When the doorbell rang she would put on the hat before opening the door. If the caller was someone she wished to see, Auntie would say how lucky it was she had just come in. If not, she would say how sorry she was to be just going out.

The Times

Every year there are rows about whether it is a good thing or a bad thing to keep moving clocks backwards and forwards for the sake of daylight saving. In the *Guardian* of 1 November 2004, the Reverend Tony Bell, of Chesterfield, Derbyshire reminded us of the man who refused to alter his clocks because the extra hour's daylight would fade his curtains.

Sir George Sitwell, father of Dame Edith, invented a small revolver specifically for shooting wasps. He used it with some success in company.

Ronald Hampton, Horncastle, Lincs,
Daily Telegraph

Sir George was an example of English eccentricity at its finest. He also invented a musical toothbrush which played *Annie Laurie* and had a notice at his home (Renishaw Hall in Derbyshire) that said: 'I must ask anyone entering the house never to contradict me in any way, as it interferes with the functioning of the gastric juices and prevents my sleeping at night.'

The Age

Simon Boyd-Wallis, of Petersfield, West Sussex, followed up the Sitwell wasp-shooting story saying 'unbeknown to most people, the wasp-shooting season starts in earnest in the summer... This exacting sport requires a .177 air pistol... A target is smeared with jam and highest points are scored only when the wasp ambles over the centre.'

Daily Telegraph

This, however, was regarded as not very British by others. 'Surely every respecting sportsman knows one does not shoot a sitting wasp. In Hampshire we shoot the driven wasp, high and fast flying.'

Daily Telegraph

'Shooting wasps is for wimps,' declared Peter Sweetman, of Madehurst, West Sussex. 'I've been safely killing the blighters with my bare hands for years. A quick nip between forefinger and thumbnail and off with their heads. Watch their back ends, though.'

Daily Telegraph

A gentler way of dealing with wasps was described by Rita Greer, of Liss, Hampshire, who told of a friend who put a teaspoon of gin in an egg-cup. He dipped a finger in the gin and extended it to the wasp. It landed on his finger and set about getting drunk. Half a minute later the wasp took off in ever-decreasing circles into the herbaceous border to sleep it off. Rita writes: 'Over the years I have used this form of wasp control...

companions sit rigid with fear and astonishment, but I have never been stung. I have tried other spirits, but gin is the favourite wasp tipple.'

Daily Telegraph

Indeed the *Daily Telegraph* disturbed a veritable nest of wasp-hunting readers. Swarms of them infested the newspaper with their own extermination solutions, which included:

- A Berloque Pistole loaded with 78rpm gramophone needles.
- A high-pressure hose.
- A swift clout with a newspaper (ideally broadsheet).
- A close-range blast of air from an air gun.
- A homemade salt pellet fired from an airgun.
- Snipping them with long-bladed scissors.

A second-hand bookstall at a church fete had a regular customer who used to buy as many books as she could carry. She said the interior walls of her bungalow were very thin and she was filling bookshelves from floor to ceiling as soundproofing. Pamela Bousfield, Bodmin, Cornwall.

The Times

When the *Guinness book of World Records* celebrated its 50th birthday in 2004, the *Independent* decided to select 'The 50 Best Record Breakers'. The second item was Mike, The Longest Surviving Headless Chicken. He survived for 18 months, being fed with an eyedropper before choking to death on a corn kernel. Among the British heroes making the Top 50 was Andy Szerbini, The Fastest Baked Bean Eater. He ate 226 baked beans in five minutes using a cocktail stick in London in 1996.

The *Daily Mirror* printed a page of the weirdest Guinness world records and, naturally, some heroic Brits earned a mention:

- The Longest Maggot Bath was endured by Christine Martin of Horsham, West Sussex – 1hr 30mins in 2002.
- Longest Time With a Nail in the Head: Robin Hanshaw, of Stoke Poges, Buckinghamshire, who had a rusty nail one-inch between his eye and ear for 22 years.
- Most One-Finger Push-Ups: Paul Lynch did 124 in London in 1922.
- Oldest Person to Loop the Loop: Adeline Ablitt, 95, did it in a glider over Leicestershire in 1998.

The 5th Duke of Portland (1800–1879) insisted that a chicken should be roasting in the kitchen at all times so he could have a hot slice whenever required.

Daily Telegraph

Brits are the world's biggest – and oddest – collectors, spending more than £500 million a year on their obsessions, reports the *Sun*.

- **Bus driver Steve Dickson, 50, of Gosport, Hampshire, collects airline sickbags.**
- **Retired civil servant John Stather, 57, collects those little sticky labels from bananas and has travelled to Helsinki, Beijing and Singapore to track down rare examples.**
- **Nick West, 45, of Clevedon, Somerset, collects beer cans. He has more than 5,000 of them and drags people in off the street to admire them.**
- **Prince Charles is potty about lavatory seats and Tara Palmer-Tomkinson collects 'Do Not Disturb' signs from hotels.**

But perhaps Britain's most obsessive collector is Tony Butcher, 44, an IT consultant from St Neots, Cambridgeshire. He has:

- over 9,000 cartoon figures on shelves in his sitting room, covering all the walls.

- 600 key rings on the walls of his entrance hall.
- limited-edition cuddly toys line up on either side of the staircase.
- 307 sweet-cigarette and candy-stick boxes and complete sets of McDonald's Mr Men.
- 900 glass bottles, 5,000 matchboxes and 100 teapot lids.
- every hand-painted Kinder Egg toy ever issued.
- a custom-made Tardis upstairs housing the complete Dr Who video set.
- Most of the ground floor is taken up by 20,000 books, with sections for comic-strip books, TV novels, TV science-fiction annuals and every Dr Who book ever issued.

Although he lives alone, he bought a four-bedroom house to have room to display his collections. And when the house is full to overflowing, he says he 'will find a way to buy the house next door'.

Sunday Telegraph

Baroness Strange – 16th in line to a title dating back to Charles I – died on 11 March 2005, aged 76. Described as engagingly eccentric and large of shape and stature, she won the affection of fellow peers and when, in 1999,

they had to elect those of the 'hereditaries' who would stay on, she was a popular choice. Her manifesto said: 'I bring flowers every week to this House from my castle in Perthshire.' She also brought bottled fruits, but they tended to explode on the flight down. The baroness worked tirelessly for good causes, including better pensions for war widows, and the family motto *Marte et Arte* (by hook or by crook) certainly applied to her.

The Times

Baroness Strange died at Megginch, her medieval castle in Perthshire. She ran a household of legendary hospitality, though there were occasional reports of guests mistaking her pet mongoose (reputed to sleep in one of her hats) for a rat.

Guardian

The 84-year-old Duchess of Devonshire is an Elvis Presley superfan, and invited Mario Kombou – star of the Presley musical show *Jailhouse Rock*, to her stately pile at Chatsworth. After enjoying scones and sandwiches (crusts removed, of course), Mario said: 'The amazing thing about her house is you see these Rembrandt paintings and then, right next to them, there'll be an Elvis telephone.' The rock star's cousin, Donna Presley, went along and reported that 'There's a sort of Elvis shrine in her bedroom.'

Independent

If he had lived (and there are many who think he still does) Elvis Presley would have been 70 in January 2005. A good enough excuse, then, for the *Daily Mail* to gather together 70 Elvis impersonators, some of whom earn around £500 an hour. The *Mail*'s picture of all 70 included an Asian from East London who admitted 'I look nothing like him' and Yorkshire housewife Enid Butler who said: 'At first it was hard being the UK's first female Elvis.'

The *Guardian* dug up Elvis Shmelvis, who calls himself Britain's only Jewish Elvis, and also reported:

- There are 22 Elvis Presleys on the UK electoral roll.
- Allied Bakeries produced special-edition loaves in the shape of Elvis's profile 'quiff and all'.
- If you key the words 'Elvis Presley' into Google, nearly three million sites come up, of which a third answer to the key words 'Elvis Lives'.

Male drivers, *see* page 45.

Chapter 13

Order, Order

MP's expenses paid with 500 mackerel...

The protestor who hit Prime Minister Tony Blair with a condom packed with purple powder, thrown from the Commons public gallery, earned this plaudit in the *Daily Telegraph*: 'It was an accurate throw from an awkward angle and would have won an admiring ripple of applause if it had been seen on the cricket field.'

After the condom had landed, Tony Blair said to Michael Howard: 'I did not set that up, you know.' The opposition leader replied: 'For once, Prime Minister, I believe you.' It was rapidly descending into a terribly British farce.

Scotsman

Health minister Stephen Ladyman told the Commons Health Committee that he experiences 'anaphylactic shock' if he encounters rats. Committee chairman David Hinchcliffe, MP, remarked: 'You've done well to get so far in this place then.'

Daily Mail

U2 front man Bono used the word 'bollocks' several times during his speech to the Labour Party's 2004 conference in Brighton. Apparently Tony Blair had been watching the chap who was interpreting speeches for the deaf and brought an uncharacteristic giggle from Gordon Brown with the question: 'What do you reckon the sign language is for bollocks?'

Daily Telegraph

'We are reviewing and updating our technical advice on walking'.
Junior Transport Minister David Jamieson, *Observer*

When it was revealed in October 2004 that the average MP's expenses cost the taxpayer £118,000, the *Daily Telegraph* took us back to the Middle Ages when parliamentarians were given expenses by their constituents to cover the cost of travelling to a session. For the member from Weymouth this took the form of 500 mackerel.

Daily Telegraph

Blunt-speaking Yorkshireman Godfrey Bloom, a UK Independence Party MEP, put himself forward as a member of the European Parliament's women's rights committee – and then horrified women MEPs by saying: 'I want to deal with women's issues because I don't think they clean behind the fridge enough. I'm here to represent Yorkshire women who always have the dinner on the table when you get home.' *Guardian*. *Times* headline: 'A woman's place is behind the fridge.'

Mr Bloom, 54, sponsors Cambridge University's ladies' rugby team and said that while some may think the rugby 'girls' manly, they 'actually scrub up very nicely'.

The Times

BBC political editor Andrew Marr in his column in the *Daily Telegraph* said he could not get out of his mind the Texan dismissal of the too-posh George Bush senior as 'the sort of man who steps out of the shower to take a piss'.

Auberon Waugh, who died aged 61 in 2001, knew Kimberly Quinn, the lady who had an affair with David Blunkett. The Ephraim Hardcastle column in the *Daily Mail* reported that when Waugh was asked if he fancied her, the satirist replied: 'Only physically.'

In 1952, when Eden was Foreign Secretary and Butler was Chancellor, the two of them arrived at Chequers demanding to see Prime Minister Churchill urgently. Winston was in bed writing a speech and told his male secretary: 'Tell them to go and bugger themselves.' As the secretary was descending the stairs to deliver the message, Churchill shouted: 'There is no need for them to carry out that instruction literally.'

Max Hastings, *Daily Mail*

One of the events that brought excitement to the beginning of 2005 was the long-awaited Freedom of Information Act and its promised release of previously withheld information. Prominent among the coverage in the nation's newspapers was the strange tale of the Home Office cat, details of which had been concealed in a file created as long ago as 1929. In the file a letter from the Treasury raised no objection to the Home Office being allowed 'to spend one penny a day from petty cash towards the maintenance of an efficient office cat.'

Guardian

Among other previously secret files was the saga of whether soft or hard loo paper was better for the bureaucratic bottom. The campaign for softer paper began in 1963 with a complaint from a Foreign Office mandarin who suffered from haemorrhoids, and in 1969 the Treasury typing pool sought help for 'us poor females' to avoid 'damage to our delicate parts'. In 1971 Her Majesty's Stationery Office warned that a switch from hard to soft paper would mean "annual expenditure on this item would shoot up from about £170,000 to between £500,000 and £835,000". A later memo said that staff should not "expect the state to mollycoddle them". Eventually, in 1981, soft rolls were permitted, and in 2005 the public were allowed a brief glimpse of life behind Civil Service lavatory doors.

Daily Telegraph

A system that locks up for 40 years information on the loo paper used by civil servants is in urgent need of a laxative.

Keith Waterhouse, quoted in the
Independent on Sunday

Gavin Robertson, of Manchester, followed up the loo-roll saga and told how his father was a civil servant during 'the hard wiping years of the 1960s and 1970s'. While all other paper was emblazoned 'On Her Majesty's Service', loo rolls were simply 'Government Property'.

Daily Telegraph

At the London County Council offices in the 1950s, typing paper carried the command: 'Please use both sides of the paper'. Some of this paper turned up in the loos 'much to the amusement of all'.

Brian O'Halloran, Pinner, Middlesex, *Daily Telegraph*

Tony Blair's key aide Jonathan Powell became embroiled in a row over whether he said to Henley Tory MP Boris Johnson that Gordon Brown would never become prime minister because he was a Scot. A delicious element of the story was that it was said to have happened when the two eminent gentlemen were on their bikes, stopped at a red light in Pall Mall. John O'Hara asked in the *Guardian* if the most unlikely part of the story wasn't the part about two cyclists stopping at a traffic light.

When the nattily dressed Anthony Eden became Prime Minister, Bertrand Russell said to Alistair Cooke: 'Not a gentleman. Dresses too well.'

The Times

When Boris Johnson, MP for Henley and editor of the *Spectator*, was appointed Shadow Arts Minister in May 2004, the *Daily Telegraph* asked him 20 arty questions. He scored seven and a half out of 20. 'I did terribly,' Johnson said: 'Ask me again after I have done a year in the job, and I'd like to think I'd get them all right.'

The *Mirror* was not impressed by the appointment and wrote of the 'Blonde mophead's barmy plans'. It pointed out that the Eton and Oxford educated shadow minister used words like 'scansion' and 'deracinating', and felt it was its duty to explain what these words mean. Scansion: To analyse the rhythm of poetry.

Deracinating: To remove someone or something from its natural environment – Boris believes we have lost our cultural roots by not studying the classic arts. All this fell under the headline: 'Bumbling MP Boris talks through his arts'.

When flying to a new post, senior diplomats are allowed to travel first class on the final leg of their journey. The Foreign Office feels this 'creates the right impression among the locals'.

Independent on Sunday

The secretive Intelligence and Security Committee deletes sensitive information from its reports with asterisks – which left one paragraph reading: 'We are concerned that *** *** *** ***. We will return to this matter.' The Government's response to this bemusing paragraph was: 'We note the committee's concern and its intention to return to the matter.'

The Times

Despite having left Parliament, former Labour minister Tony Benn still harbours plans to put republicanism into effect. He says: 'I haven't renounced my membership of the Privy Council because I would like to live to see it meet.' The Council meets only on the demise of the monarch and its declaration of the succession is traditionally signed 'with one heart and mind and voice'.

Benn says this 'is what is known as the unanimity rule, so if I wrote "No" the Crown would not be proclaimed.'

Independent on Sunday

Tony Benn had to battle hard and long to shed his hereditary title of Viscount Stansgate. The Peerage Act of 1963 made it possible for him to do so (and to become an MP again). He remembers rushing to the Lord Chancellor's Office with his Instrument of Renunciation and how the man on the door greeted him on his way in with 'Good afternoon, my Lord.' On Benn's way out, the doorman said: 'Goodbye, sir.' From Benn's memoirs *Dare to be a Daniel.*

Daily Mail

'The Opening of Parliament has become one of those ancient rituals which the British do so well – or so we always tell ourselves,' wrote Simon Hoggart in the *Guardian*. He told of 'massed ambassadors looking just like envoys in a film about Ruritania' and 'law lords sitting on the Woolsack, like the haul of Saturday night tarts in a Parisian paddy wagon.'

During the Swinging Sixties the BBC received a letter from a 20-year-old Sheffield student who was irate about naked bodies being shown on prime-time TV. It was only after they invited him down to London to take part in a televised debate with Mary

Whitehouse and David Dimbleby that they discovered that student David Blunkett was blind.

Independent on Sunday

At a time when newspapers were full of the story of Home Secretary David Blunkett's love affair (and before his resignation on 14 December 2004) Andrew Alexander reminded *Daily Mail* readers that in Victorian times:

- Lord Palmerston was a highly successful Home Secretary, Foreign Secretary and Prime Minister. He was also a woman chaser, and said to have died in flagrante. It was also rumoured that he once tried to break down a door in Windsor Castle in pursuit of an assignation (he had got the wrong room).
- Gladstone was renowned as a virtuous Prime Minister. But all those late-night walks to rescue fallen women, while apparently estimable, were accompanied by self-flagellation – suggesting less than 100 per cent innocence.
- Asquith, who presided over the great reforming Liberal administration of the early 1900s, had a mistress to whom he wrote notes during Cabinet meetings.

Former Labour minister Tony Banks announced in 2004 that he was standing down after two decades in Westminster. He said his work as MP for West Ham had been 'tedious in the extreme'. He had found his constituents' problems boring and had got no satisfaction from helping them.

Daily Telegraph

After winning the 2001 election Labour's senior ministers went to Buckingham Palace to receive their seals of office. One of those present said: 'We were dead on our feet after campaigning for three weeks... John Prescott kneeled, recited his oath and walked away leaving the Queen still holding his seals of office. Jack Straw mangled his oath – then steered blind David Blunkett towards the Queen. Blunkett ended up facing not the Queen, but a statue of George IV – to which he addressed his oath. At the end of a shambolic series of events, the Queen said: "I hope you run the country better than you have managed over the last 15 minutes."'

Extracted from Stephen Pollard's biography of David Blunkett, *Daily Mail*

When he was an MP, Gyles Brandreth used to be a Lord Commissioner of HM Treasury. This involves the signing of a cheque at general election time which allows government spending to continue when there isn't a parliament to vote on the money.

In 1997 the cheque was for £136 *billion*. The Queen has to countersign the cheque so Gyles was driven to Buckingham Palace and ushered into the presence. He looked on as the Queen signed and then said: 'The fact that we have to countersign this, your majesty, makes me wonder which one of us they don't trust.'

Simon Hoggart, *Guardian*

It's one of the most famous doors in the world – that of No.10 Downing Street. So the *Guardian* decided to post a photographer outside it for a whole day. His reward was photo-opportunities of: four cabinet ministers, three world leaders, two senior European diplomats, some visiting schoolchildren from Morecambe, a former BBC director general, Ian Paisley, a street sweeper, some academics and captains of business arriving for breakfast, Cherie Blair, deliveries of dry-cleaning, sandwiches from Marks & Spencer and editions of the *Evening Standard*, and a delegation of MPs from the All-Party Parliamentary Historic Vehicles Club. The solitary policeman on guard said: 'I wouldn't say I switch off, exactly. I prefer to say that I'm like a coiled spring.' At 7.40pm a fox strolled across the No.10 doorway – possibly, said the *Guardian*, to convey its gratitude for the government's ban on hunting.

When former US president Bill Clinton turned up for a book-signing session (*My Life*, by Bill Clinton) at Waterstone's in Piccadilly, they placed him between Fantasy and Crime and directly facing Erotica.

The Times

Letter from Lady Roberts, of Hereford: 'My late husband used to wear a bowler when he worked in the Foreign Office in the late 1960s. One Budget Day he was attacked by an elderly lady with an umbrella who thought he was the Chancellor of the Exchequer.'

The Times

The Monster Raving Loony Party was founded in 1963. Its manifesto included the vote at 18, local radio stations and all-day pub opening.

Daily Mail

Macbeth was not the murderous villain portrayed by Shakespeare. He was a cuddly, successful, peace-loving king say members of the Scottish Parliament. The MSPs want to rescue the 11th century monarch from his 'bad press' and see 2005 (the 1,000th anniversary of his birth) as the year in which he acquires a new halo – and boosts tourism.

The Times

On 10 February 2005 the Queen inaugurated the Churchill Museum – next to the underground Cabinet War Rooms where the great man conducted much of World War II. Exhibits include one of his cerise-coloured siren suits, his pork-pie hat and polka-dot bow tie, his christening robe and baby rattle. There is also a half-smoked cigar which is believed to be authentic because civil servants used to pick up discarded butts as souvenirs.

Guardian

On the same day newspapers reported a poll which revealed that many teenagers thought that Churchill was an insurance salesman. Secondary school pupils were confusing the inspirational leader with the nodding bulldog used in TV ads by Churchill Insurance.

Sun/Daily Mail

New police tactics to beat crime, *see* page 56.

Chapter 14

Service Life

Pots, chamber, crested, admirals for the use of.
Pots, chamber, rubber, lunatics for the use of...

Speaking at the 2004 Derby Club dinner at the Savoy, Shadow Defence spokesman Nicholas Soames recalled the final stages of his officer training. The day before being commissioned, his Regimental Sergeant Major said: 'Tomorrow, Soames, you will have one pip on your left shoulder and one pip on your right shoulder. I shall have to address you as 'Sir'. But deep down I shall always think of you as a complete and utter c***.'

Independent on Sunday

The secret weapon used by SAS jungle fighters against mosquitoes is Avon ladies' hand cream. Others use Marmite because mosquitoes hate its odour.

Sun

In my Territorial days, while engaged in TEWTS (exercises without troops), the padre would conduct BEWBS (Burial Exercises Without Bodies).
  Peter Brisbourne, Brentwood, Essex, *Daily Telegraph*

Michael Bacon of Farnham, Surrey, followed this up with another training standby, NEWD, which stood for Night Exercise Without Darkness.

Daily Telegraph

British soldiers training for Iraq had to shout "Bang!" instead of firing their hand-grenade launchers because the MoD didn't buy enough.

Daily Telegraph

While working at the Admiralty during World War II, Mercia Mason culled the following stores terminology from Fleet Orders:

- Pots, chamber, crested, admirals for the use of.
- Pots, chamber, rubber, lunatics for the use of. *The Times*

New Irish Guards recruit Martyn Walters is 7ft 3ins and too tall to fit in sentry boxes outside royal palaces when he wears his bearskin. He will be replaced by a shorter soldier when it rains.

The Times

This story reminds the author of Spike Milligan's joke about his diminutive father getting into the Irish Guards by lying about his height.

In December 2004 there were celebrations to commemorate the 60th anniversary of the date that the Home Guard stood down. Portrayed as Dad's Army in the long-running BBC TV series, the real-life volunteer force was set up in the darkest days of World War II and equipped with enthusiasm and a strange array of weapons, including home-made pikes. It became one of the greatest successes of democratic mobilisation, but 'sometimes frightened the British authorities as much as it alarmed Adolf Hitler'.

Guardian

Our local church fete included an Army demonstration of unarmed combat. Soldiers with heavily protected forearms were attacked by cudgel-wielding comrades who were quickly disarmed and flung to the ground. A little boy was invited to have a go, but he ignored the

protected forearm and banged the PTI sergeant on the shins, leaving the NCO roaring with pain.

Maurice Cross, Keynsham, Bristol, *Daily Mail*

The budget for feeding the crew of *HMS Monmouth* works out at £2.80 a day each. It is on an anti-drugs mission in the Caribbean, along with a sniffer dog called Casper. The cost of feeding Casper is £3.

Sunday Telegraph

Chapter 15

Sporting Life

**Jockey Club says Cupid Stunt is no
name for a race horse...**

The Plain English Campaign defended football
commentators who make Colemanballs-style gaffes,
reminding us that they have to speak at great speed.
Nevertheless, *The Times* could not resist reminding us
of some gems:

- Football's football. If that weren't the case it
  wouldn't be the game that it is – Garth
  Crooks
- The World Cup... a truly international event –
  John Motson
- The most vulnerable area for goalies is
  between their legs – Andy Gray

- **Southampton have forced Manchester United into a lot of unforced errors – Steve Claridge**
- **He sliced the ball when he had it on a plate – Ron Atkinson**
- **If England get a point, it will be a point gained as opposed to two points lost – Mark Lawrenson**
- **That shot might not have been as good as it might have been – John Motson**
- **Thistle will need to score at least once if they want to win this game – Sandy Clark**
- **He's treading on dangerous water here – Ron Atkinson**

John Sharkey watched some ladies' football matches during the 2004 Olympics and commented: 'The game they played was 20 years out of date. They did not spit. They did not dive. They did not fall down whenever they were in the penalty area. They did not feign injury. There was no arguing with the referee... There were no really nasty tackles. They have a long way to go to catch up with our highly paid professionals. Long may it be so.'

Independent

Ally Ross, the *Sun's* TV columnist, wrote of 'the battle to produce the most moronic Euro 2004 coverage' and made an early selection:

- 'If I had to play one person on the left it would be Ashley Cole and Wayne Bridge' – Peter Beardsley on Sky
- Best Mixed Metaphor: 'It's a different kettle of fish if Sven doesn't take the bull by the horns, 'cos he'll end up painting himself into a corner.'

He also recorded a Great Sporting Insight from Dave Jones, manager of struggling Wolverhampton Wanderers: 'We're hoping against hope it isn't hopeless.'

'Aston Villa are seventh in the League. That's almost as high as you can get without being one of the top six.'

Ian Payne, *Radio Five Live*

Sohail Rasul, of New Malden, Surrey, told *The Times* that he was delighted that Middlesex have a bowler named Batt and Somerset have a batsman named Bowler. 'I look forward to hearing the commentary: 'Bowler is batting and Batt is bowling.'

This recalls the Brian Johnston Test match classic when Peter Willey of England bowled to Michael Holding of the West Indies at the Oval in 1976: 'The batsman's Holding, the bowler's Willey'.

Private Eye and many others

'The galactic stupidity of footballers never fails to amaze me sometimes.'

Rodney Marsh, quoted in the *Sun*

I queued for a steaming hot pie at the Old Trafford football ground in Manchester and asked if I might have a fork. 'You want a fork?' asked the incredulous man behind the counter. 'Southerner, are you?'

Jim White in the *Daily Telegraph*.

The Jockey Club has strict rules about the naming of racehorses but the occasional dodgy one slips through. 'Country Member' was a noteworthy failure for the Club's censorship procedures. One called 'Big Tits' made it after being cleared by the French, and Noble Locks also got through. Saucy names blocked in the past include Sofa King Fast, Cupid Stunt, Norfolk Enchants, Sparrowfaht, Ah Feic and Fog Ducker.

Independent/Sun/Jockey Club

BBC commentator John Motson unwittingly cost bookmakers thousands of pounds with one of his trademarks football clichés. One available bet was on which one Motson would use first during the Euro 2004 match between England and Portugal. Many chose 'These are anxious moments'. The game was only 69 seconds old when John uttered the words.

Sunday Times

The *Sunday Times* recalled some famous 'Mottyisms' including:

- 'The goals made such a difference to the way this game went.'
- 'The match has become quite unpredictable, but it still looks as though Arsenal will win the cup.'
- 'For those of you watching in black and white, Spurs are in the all-yellow strip.'

A book called *The Gaffta Awards* records some classic quotes from England's football legends:

- 'We didn't underestimate them – they were just better than we thought' – Sir Bobby Robson
- 'I've had 14 bookings. Eight were my fault, but seven were disputable' – Paul Gascoigne
- 'He dribbles a lot. The opposition don't like it. You can see it all over their faces' – Ron Atkinson
- 'There's great harmonium in the dressing room' – Sir Alf Ramsey

Reporting on an injured football player: 'His absence will undoubtedly be sorely missed.'

Spotted in the *Exeter Express and Echo*
by Nigel Power of Exeter

After a dismal run of failures Norwich City's football team were advised by local psychic Samanda Chambers to wear red underpants. Norwich fan Samanda promised to wear red knickers at future games and said: 'Red is the colour of positivity. The groin is where the emotions are held. Wearing red here increases feelings of inner worth.'

Sun/Seattle Times (There is no confirmation that the players took Samanda's advice but Norwich ended up being relegated.)

Ladies' Day at Ascot used to be devoted to the beauty of Britain's fairer sex. Today, it's about as stylish and classy as a hen night during happy hour... with hats that look as though the Labrador recently gave birth in them. There are some truly lovely visions to behold. Unfortunately for humanity most of them are in the paddocks.

The Times fashion editor Lisa Armstrong

The Dowager Lady Killearn, 88, arrived at Ascot in her vintage Rolls Royce saying: 'Standards have slipped so much. Some women aren't even wearing hats. It's just too terrible.'

Daily Telegraph

Ascot ladies were able to watch England beat Switzerland at football on a big-screen TV and the *Daily Mail* reported 'an authentic Eliza Doolittle moment as one serene symphony in pink lost her poise and bellowed: "C'mon, Becks! Move your arse!"'

There are six times as many people in the public spaces as in the Ascot Royal Enclosure. But far from making the event more meritocratic, the expansion merely underlines the class divisions... The toffs laugh at the proles; the proles sneer at the toffs.

Guardian

Westgate Hammers football club in Kent will keep Wally the parrot as its mascot despite its demise. The ex-parrot will be stuffed.

Sun

Ellen MacArthur's triumphant, record-breaking sail around the world was not a 100 per cent PR success for her sponsors B&Q.

- Jackie Smith of Manchester pointed out that it had taken B&Q longer to install her kitchen than it took the brave lady sailor to circumnavigate the globe. *Daily Telegraph*
- B&Q were said to have received this

155

email within hours of Ms MacArthur arriving back home: 'My congratulations to you on getting a yacht to leave the UK on 28th November 2004, sail 27,354 miles around the world and arrive back 72 days later. Could you please let me know when the kitchen I ordered 96 days ago will be arriving from your warehouse 13 miles away?' This was later reported to be an Internet spoof by BBC's *Watchdog* programme.

There have been some 35 recorded small-boat solo circumnavigations since 1895. Probably the slowest was that of Edward Allcard in his old 26ft wooden ketch *Temptress*. It took him 16 years.

David Simpson, Barry, Vale of Glamorgan
Daily Telegraph

Between overs, while fielding at deep mid off last Sunday, I picked about half a pound of wild mushrooms.

Alan Dawson, Diss, Norfolk, *The Times*

One of our players was on his mobile while fielding on the boundary. An opposition batsman hit a huge shot high in the air. Our fieldsman told his caller to hold on, put the phone in his pocket, took an excellent catch, then retrieved his phone and resumed his conversation as if nothing had happened. Jim Strother, St. Albans, Herts.

Daily Telegraph

Another cricketing 'champagne moment'. At a match on the common at Tunbridge Wells a deep fielder, vaguely conscious of having heard a loud click from the direction of the wicket, looked up to see a small, dark shape hurtling towards him. Instinctively his hand shot up and, in one of the neatest catches ever witnessed on the common, he caught a swallow. Jonathan Goodall, Bath, Somerset.

Daily Telegraph

The gloves worn by Henry Cooper when he fought Muhammad Ali in 1966 were auctioned in 2004 for £19,000. 'That's more than I got for the bleeding fight,' said Henry.

Observer

England manager Sven-Göran Eriksson says in *Square Meal* magazine that football, the beautiful game, 'is like the Colosseum was 2,000 years ago... Then spectators watched Christians and lions for entertainment. Today football is the show they want. It is normal to see usually smart and elegant men shouting passionately at the referee... That is so beautiful.'

The Times

Chris Bell, chief executive of Ladbrokes, UK's biggest book-maker, claims that at least one horse race a day is fixed.

Independent

Hottest-selling lines produced by Subbuteo accessories dealer Tom Taylor are male and female streakers – along with police officers with helmets ready for a strategic cover up. Tom, who has a shop and workroom in the Welsh border town of Knighton, says his nude models are 'anatomically perfect'.

The Times/Daily Express

A greyhound called Simply Fabulous, fed on bangers and mash, beat a racehorse called Tiny Tim in a two-furlong dash at Kempton Park. The horse had been the bookies' favourite and one punter bet £11,000 that it would win. Biggest bet on the dog was £200.

Daily Telegraph

A bookie in Putney, London, hired a feng shui expert to redesign its betting shop – because punters keep on winning.

Sun

Former England striker Gary Lineker gets up to £25,000 as an after-dinner speaker. Among the things he says is: 'Football is a simple game. Twenty-two men chase a ball for 90 minutes and, at the end, the Germans win.'

Independent on Sunday

Wimbledon is being forced to increase the size of its Centre Court seats to accommodate ever-fatter spectators. The original seats measure between 40cm and 42cm and were installed in 1922 when tennis fans were considerably slimmer. The new seats will be a minimum 46cm.

The Times

Not many holds were barred in the rough, tough Olympic games played in England in the 17th century. Competitors were sometimes seriously injured or even killed. In one contest a Mr Hutchinson cut off the nose of Sir German Poole, picked it up, put it in his pocket and went off with it so that it could not be sewn on again. Extract from Celia Haddon's book *The First Ever English Olimpick Games*, in *The Times* under the headline: 'A very English Olympics'.

Beckham missed a penalty, England went out of Euro 2004 – and David found himself the butt of 'a million internet jokes'. One of them had the England football captain accepting this advice from Rugby World Cup hero Jonny Wilkinson: 'To win, just kick the ball over the bar.'

The Times

Michael Owen, who scored a goal against Portugal, said: 'These tournaments only come round every two years but you can't expect to win it every year.'

Sun

England lost at football and Henman lost by three straight sets at Wimbledon. But the *Sun* sought to cheer its readers up by reminding them that the Brits are masters at the zany sport of extreme ironing and also the world's tiddlywinks champions.

It was reported that, during a row, the fiancée of footballing ace Wayne Rooney, threw her £25,000 engagement ring into a wood in Formby on Merseyside. People who turned up hoping to find the ring were banned from searching the wood – for fear of harming rare red squirrels.

Guardian

At Lord's cricket ground I was asked to surrender a bottle opener incorporating a small penknife. However, once inside the ground, I was able to buy at the Lord's Cricket Shop another bottle opener with a similar blade.

Andrew Durrant London, W6, *The Times*

Who did you think you were kidding Mr. Hitler? As Britain faced its darkest hour in 1940 the nation's golfers knew how to cope with a spot of warfare and were advised thus: 'In competition, during gunfire or while bombs are falling, players may take cover without penalty for ceasing play. The positions of known delayed action bombs are marked by red flags at a reasonably, but not guaranteed, safe distance therefrom... A ball

moved by enemy action may be replaced, or, if lost or destroyed, a ball may be dropped not nearer the hole without a penalty. A player whose stroke is affected by the simultaneous explosion of a bomb may play another ball from the same place. Penalty, one stroke.'

Temporary Rules 1940, Richmond Golf Club

Sometimes football IS the beautiful game. In a Yeovil Town v Plymouth Argyle cup match Yeovil scored in a misunderstanding, so the Town manager told his players to let Plymouth roll in a goal to level the match. His sportsmanship was rewarded – Yeovil went on to win 3–2.

Sun

Brian Clough – 'the greatest football manager England never had' – died in September 2004. Just about every newspaper in the land carried fulsome obituaries and samples of his 'wit and wisdom'.

- 'I wouldn't say I was the best manager in the business. But I was in the top one.'
- On Sven-Göran Eriksson becoming England manager: 'At last they have one who speaks English better than the players.'
- On dealing with a player who disagrees: 'We talk about it for 20 minutes and then we decide I was right.'

John Burns, 33, became the 2004 World Black Pudding Throwing Champion when the international event was staged at the Royal Oak pub in Ramsbottom, Lancashire. In the contest, six-ounce Lancashire black puddings swaddled in ladies' tights are hurled underarm at a pile of Yorkshire puddings. John, who knocked over seven puddings with a single throw, said later: 'This is not going to change me.'

Bury News/BBC Manchester

During a cricket match between Boldon and Marsden in the Durham Senior League, a ball passed between the stumps without dislodging the bails. The remarkable let-off cost Boldon the league title.

Daily Mirror

Ben Fish, for many years question master of the Shropshire Cricket Association quiz, would make it clear at the start that 'the answer I'm looking for is not necessarily the correct one, but the one I have here on the card.'

Mike Robinson, Oswestry, Shropshire, *The Times*

Mike Claughton, of Ashford, Kent, recalled a quiz in which competitors were asked what you were afraid of if you suffered from taphophobia. A few knew the answer (a dread of being buried alive). But a spot prize was awarded to the team which offered 'a very plausible alternative' – a morbid fear of Welshmen.

The Times

Online betting firm Betfair gave 29 newspaper sports desk teams £250 to gamble over ten days. Twenty-three of them finished with less money than they started with. Seven completely lost their shirts – among them the Racing Post. Of the six teams that made a profit, *The Times* won with a final pot of £750.

Press Gazette

The *Guardian* diary apologised for reminding Portsmouth football fans that the name of their ground (Fratton Park) reads backwards as Krap, Nott Arf.

The girlfriend of football fan Simon Bowen was not best pleased at the Christmas tree he provided. It was sprayed black and gold – the colours of Wolverhampton Wanderers – and pictures of the team's players were hanging from the branches.

Sunday Times

The Scottish football team's world ranking sank to an all-time low of 77th in 2004. But at the end of the year, the Scots were holding their heads high as world champions – at elephant polo. (It is a foul if an elephant lies down in front of the goal or picks up the ball with its trunk.)

East Lothian Courier/Times/Guardian

Scotland has had an elephant polo team since 1983 when the sport – now registered with the Olympics, was co-founded by Scot James Manclark. When the team returned from Nepal in December, their captain, the Duke of Argyll, said: 'With this victory no one can deny Scotland are one of the world's sporting heavyweights.'

Guardian

It was a time for celebration when the under-13s soccer team from Upwell, in Norfolk, suffered a 7–1 defeat against the Reffley Rovers in the Mid-Norfolk League. It was the first time they had scored a goal during the season – having conceded 136 goals in nine games. A team official rejoiced, saying: 'It was a great moment for the whole team.'

Evening Standard

Chelsea's pampered football stars decided there was something missing from their £20 million training set-up at Cobham, Surrey. Their luxury complex already included better facilities than most five-star hotels (including a state of the art gym and health suite) but the players wanted a bank of sun beds to top up their tans.

Sun

Manchester United players, meanwhile, had heated bootpegs installed at their Carrington training ground –

164

'to keep their tootsies warm' and Arsenal stars are having a beauty parlour built in their new Ashburton Grove ground.

Sun

When the local team at Alton were defeated in a big cup match, the *Farnham Herald's* headline was 'Alton bow out with heads held high'.

Golf is 'naff... racist... class ridden... snobbish... sexist... tedious to watch... a fundamentally stupid game,' wrote A.A. Gill in *GQ* magazine. A spokesman for St Andrews Golf Club responded by saying that the fact that the game has survived 600 years 'tends to indicate it is a sport a great number of people find extremely fulfilling.'

Independent **Pandora column**

Football leagues across the country are in turmoil because of violence, foul language and abuse of referees. But it's not the behaviour of professionals being complained about – it's that of parents attending children's leagues. In January 2005 it was reported that the FA was investigating 100 cases in which adult spectators were accused of abusing or attacking players, officials and parental spectators. Parents even shout and swear at their own children and some have been banned from travelling on the team bus. Even girls' matches have become battlegrounds. At one Essex event for girls under

13, parents got involved in a fight and one drove his car onto the pitch and began wielding a spade. Police were called and made an arrest.

Observer

In February 2005 the International Olympic Committee came to see if London should host the 2012 Games. Tanya Gold in the *Guardian* offered '40 incontrovertible reasons why London trounces the French capital any day'. They included:

- Some public Parisian public toilets have glossy brass coathooks and oval mirrors. This is insufferable grandeur. London toilets are honest, decent toilets. Their mirrors are cracked, there is no paper and they smell. Just as it should be.
- London cab drivers are masters of conversational charm. They are avid gossips and keen surveyors of the political landscape. If you tip them they will not swear at you.
- London SE18 features a Ha Ha Road. There was once a ditch there. When Londoners fell in other Londoners would shout 'Ha! Ha!' This is actually true.
- Londoners can still drive geese and swine through Dulwich, if they pay the tolls. Parisians would doubtless kidnap, force-feed and eat the ducks.

Guardian

A football match arranged to promote racial harmony in Swansea turned into a brawl. The game, between the Swansea All Stars and a side called Toofan, had to be abandoned. 'Everyone went crazy,' the court was told. 'Everyone was fighting and shouting.'

Daily Telegraph

British golfer Max Faulkner, OBE, died aged 88 in February 2005. He won the 1951 Open Championship but was as famous for his colourful dress and mischievous sense of humour as for his golf. He used to milk cows to build up strength in his wrists and walk on his hands from green to tee.

Times **obituary**

Soccer legend Kevin Keegan quit Manchester City in March 2005 and the Sun reported that fans would mourn his leaving because the 54-year-old may no longer have a platform 'at what he does best – open his mouth and put his foot in it'. Under the headline 'Keeganballs' it printed half a page of 'some of the best of Kev's crazy quotes':

- 'England have the best fans in the world and Scotland's fans are second to none.'
- 'We deserved to win this game by hammering them 0–0 in the first half.'
- 'That decision was, for me, almost certainly definitely wrong.'

- 'That would have been a goal if it wasn't saved.'
- 'The game has gone rather scrappy as both sides realise they could win this match or lose it.'

Football was never intended as a 'beautiful game', but was developed as a brute exercise in manliness aimed at preventing Victorian schoolboys from succumbing to reckless immorality. *The Times* reporting on David Winner's *book Those Feet: A Sensual History of England Football.*

Chapter 16

A Touch of Class

Favoured visitors invited to see Duke's colourful private parts...

In an article about good manners Thomas Blaikie recalled the story of an Edwardian hostess who was showing 'a particularly virginal girl' around the house. They came across a couple bonking on the floor and the hostess said: 'Ah, mending the carpet. How kind!'

Independent on Sunday

The only truly classless places in Britain are... boot sales. A study by the research body Demos has identified three distinct UK types who frequent the sales – people who would never mix in any other setting. The first are the low-income bargain-hunters who go along to take advantage of cheap household goods. The second are the 'fashionista bohos' looking for stylish nick-nacks and vintage records. The third are the 'middle Englanders' – affluent people looking for treasures among the junk.

Independent on Sunday

At the launch of his new book *Blenheim and the Churchills*, Hugh Montgomery-Massingberd told how the 10th Duke of Marlborough used to have a secret garden. He liked to tell favoured visitors: 'You must see my private parts. They are very colourful at this time of year.'

Daily Mail

Julian Fellowes, author of the novel *Snobs,* writes in the *Daily Mail* that the Duke of Rutland, when asked if he ever ate dinner without changing to white tie, replied: 'Only when we dine alone in the wife's bedroom.'

Julian's wife Emma admits to being riveted by the nuances of snobbery and casts an expert eye over everything her husband writes. She says: 'Sometimes, I'm ashamed to say, I'll go upstairs after a dinner party and say to Julian: 'Did you see Cybilla tipping her soup towards her?'

Daily Telegraph

Emma tells the story of Julian inviting American friends to a dinner party and saying: 'I hope you don't mind, but we're dressing up.' Everyone turned up in black tie until the Americans arrived. He was dressed as Frankenstein's monster with dripping blood and a bolt through his neck. She was in a miniskirt as a sexy nurse.

Daily Telegraph

A new version of the *Oxford Dictionary of National Biography* was published in September 2004. It has 62.5 million words, 60,305 pages, 60 volumes and costs £7,500. Sales are not expected to cover the £30 million cost of producing it. It includes:

- A 'warts and all' entry on Diana, Prince of Wales, which says: 'A popular, essentially jolly girl with a talent for making friends, she had no academic success (twice failing all her O levels). But, arguably, none was required for girls of her class who had no need to earn a living; indeed, displays of intellect could be frowned upon by the largely Philistine county set.' *Daily Telegraph*
- An entry on Sir Charles Isham, 'the probable father of the garden gnome... who grew interested in tiny beings he thought lived underground. He placed hand-modelled gnomes wielding spades and pick axes and

pushing wheelbarrows in his rockery at
Lamport – as though they were mining it.'
Guardian
- The *Daily Mail's* review of the book says it is
a reminder that we are really a race of
eccentrics, neurotics and sometimes
downright rotters.

Esquire magazine gave etiquette advice for modern
men and included how to behave in a public
lavatory.

- At the urinal it is 'eyes up' at all times –
  except when your neighbour is a
  celebrity when a surreptitious glance
  is fine.
- Whistling is fine at the urinal and the
  washbasin, but not in the cubicle.
- Singing is fine at the basin, but nowhere
  else.
- Texting is OK in the cubicle but not at
  the urinal or basin.

The *Daily Mail* followed *Esquire* with a similar guide for
women and advised: 'When in the sauna or steam room
keep your knees together, your feet on the ground, your
eyes on the floor and your hands clasped in your lap at
all times.'

Members of the Reform Club are to vote on a change in the club rules. They are being asked to approve using the words 'member of the staff' instead of 'servant'.

Guardian/Sunday Telegraph

Members of the men-only Beefsteak Club – a notable pillar of the Establishment – call all their waiters 'Charles', which saves them having to remember their real names. The Club was founded in 1876, and in its early days was once raided by police who mistook it for a brothel. The first member to be interviewed told police he was the Prime Minister. 'Oh yes,' said the officer to another member. 'And I suppose you're the Archbishop of Canterbury?' 'As a matter of fact, I am,' was the reply.

Richard Kay's column in the *Daily Mail*

The Cockermouth Conservative Club in Cumbria has barred women becoming full members because the men's language is too blue. In April 2004 the club voted against the women for the second time because male members would need to curb their language in the bar.

Daily Telegraph

Musing about the possibility of a classless society, Sir Peregrine Worsthorne writes that if he were to be deprived of his knighthood '...the difference will be the lifting of a small burden of moral obligation to give a

rather larger tip than had been my wont before I was knighted.' From an extract of his book *In Defence of Aristocracy* (Harper Collins).

Guardian

Middle England is in terminal decline and its traditional values of self-reliance are in retreat, according to social commentator Digby Anderson in a provocative report called *All Oiks Now*, published by the right-wing think tank, the Social Affairs Unit. He says middle-class, middle-aged people are 'desperately apeing the dress and manners of the lower classes and 'yoof'.

The Times

Lady Borthwick, of Heriot, Midlothian, responded to Anderson's report with a letter to the *Daily Telegraph*, saying: 'Sadly, anyone speaking the Queen's English is now derided as a toff... Many of your recent obituaries have been about men and women who served this country with pride. They have had their eccentricities and quirks, but are not these characteristics that we expect from a true Brit?'

Nigel Bowley, of London NW1 wrote of Middle England's surrender to oik 'culture' and said: 'Politeness is now seen only as a weakness... These days people say sorry just before jumping a queue.'

Daily Telegraph

Sir Peregrine Worsthorne, 'former editor of the *Sunday Telegraph* and unashamed snob', does not think the classless society is a good idea. He thinks we should teach the sons and daughters of the very rich how to govern us. 'Of all the aristocracies in Europe,' he says, 'ours was the most successful, the most long lasting and civilised. We mustn't consign its virtues to the dustbin.'

Interviewed in The Times

Auberon Waugh used to say: 'We never don black tie (as opposed to white tie) unless dining with the middle class.

Diarist Christopher Silvester,
Independent on Sunday

In the early 18th century 'Beau' Nash transformed Bath into the resort of choice for 'polite society'. He developed a code of behaviour that encouraged sociability between the growing gentry class and the aristocratic elite who had traditionally kept themselves apart from the rest of society. One of the rules of the code was 'that no gentlemen give tickets to balls to any but gentlewomen. NB – unless he has none of his acquaintance.'

From the *Museum of Costume & Assembly Rooms, Bath: The Official Guide*

Letter in the *Times* from 'An Old Etonian': 'Sir, Today's Young Men. More than ever before in the history of youth do they defy discipline and worship independence, brush aside experience and do exactly as they please'. The letter appeared in August 1921.

Sir Norman Wisdom – the Queen's favourite funny man – announced that he would retire when he reached 90 in February 2005. He came from a broken home and, as a grubby-kneed urchin, used to steal to survive. The flat-capped clown was once taken to Simpson's in the Strand, ordered tinned salmon and was disappointed to find that they served only the fresh version.

Quentin Letts, *Daily Mail*

Chapter 17

Council Daze

**Warden slaps ticket on mangled moped as
injured rider is carried into ambulance...**

Dog fouling continues to anger Isle of Axholme
councillors – and they aim to stamp down hard on it.

Scunthorpe Telegraph

Disabled pensioner Frank Hayward was given a
parking ticket in Southampton because his car's
disabled badge was covered by frost.

Sun

Harry Sas, of Clevedon, Somerset, complained to his council that his street was dirty. He was sent a broom, a litter picker and binliners so that he could do the job himself.

BBC News/Daily Telegraph

Krister Nylander lives in Sweden and has a snowmobile. He has never been to Warwick and was therefore surprised to receive a £90 ticket for illegally parking his snowmobile there in June – especially as the vehicle depends on the presence of snow in order to get about. Mr Nylander said: 'They can wait till hell freezes over and I can get to Britain on my snowmobile to pay the fine.'

The Times

Headline writers often have trouble coping with Britain's oddball place names. The West Dorset District Council's Community Link newsletter carried this one: 'Piddle scheme to protect homes from flooding.' Spotted by C. Basham, Lyme Regis, Dorset.

Daily Mail

Wasps got drunk and became aggressive on the fermentation from rotting fruit that had fallen from a pear tree. Birmingham's solution? Chop the tree down.

Guardian

Temporary traffic lights have delayed drivers on the A483, north of Llanbadarn Fynydd, Powys, since 1997 because of a row over who should pay for extra work. In June 2004 Liberal MP Roger Williams commented: 'The lights have been there so long that they have become a tourist attraction'.

Sunday Times

Businessman Geoffrey Torkington was owed £485,000 by Salford Council. He got his money after sending bailiffs to the town hall.

Sun

Milkman Graham O'Keeffe, who delivers in Soho, got 40 parking tickets in six months. One of the £50 fines was imposed at 7.20am.

Daily Mail

Council workers in Hull bounced Steve Tether's car away from the kerb so that they could paint double yellow lines on the road. They then bounced it back and a traffic warden slapped a £30 penalty ticket on the windscreen. The council cancelled the ticket after Steve complained.

Sun

Westminster council's plan to crack down on Soho's brothels and clip joints is being opposed by Sohemians, a society pledged to protect Soho's heritage as

'London's most louche and colourful neighbourhood'. The society says the council 'will not be satisfied until they have transformed Soho into yet another bland, dreary residential area. So-called clip joints and brothels are an integral part of Soho's life.'

Guardian

Artist Tom Bloor spent nine hours pasting pop-art wallpaper over a city-centre walkway in Birmingham as part of a visual arts event. He did it with the blessing of the city council which had been awarded £2 million to promote urban culture. Next day Mr Bloor found that council workers had scrubbed off his subway art after mistaking it for fly-posting.

Birmingham Post/Guardian

Manchester City Council's budget for repairing broken pavements is smaller than the amount it spends on compensation claims from people who fall over on broken pavements.

Daily Mail

Removal man Tony Hilton has protested to Westminster Council that a traffic warden gave him a £100 parking ticket – while he was stuck in a traffic jam. He complained that the jam had been caused... by a Westminster council lorry.

Sun

Blue lights were flashing. Police and paramedics were scurrying about. A moped rider was writhing in agony after crashing and breaking a leg. The rider was stretchered into an ambulance, but a traffic warden slapped a £100 penalty notice onto the mangled moped – and earned the award for 'The Craziest Parking Ticket of the Year' from AppealNow.com, an organisation lobbying for sanity and fairness. (The ticket was later rescinded by Lambeth council.)

The Times

Mrs Ellen Geary, 49, parked in a road without yellow lines in Bournemouth. At 4.30pm, while she was away, workmen came along and painted yellow lines which finished at the rear of her car – and re-started from the front of it. At 4.45pm a warden came along and slapped a ticket on her windscreen. Mrs Geary said the warden 'could have used some common sense rather than be the plonker of the year.'

Daily Mail

Victoria Annand, 26, parked in a Birkenhead car park and then went to the parking ticket machine. There was a queue and it took seven minutes to get a ticket. When she got back to her car a warden was already writing out a £60 penalty fine. She told Victoria that motorists were allowed only five minutes to buy tickets and she was two minutes past the deadline. Wirral council cancelled the ticket after an investigation.

Daily Mail

A 15-year-old Peugeot was illegally parked and apparently abandoned in Sale, Greater Manchester, on 7 January 2005. By 8 February 2005 it had collected nearly 30 parking tickets collectively worth £1,680 – about ten times the value of the car.

Sun

Motorists who parked legally in Windsor Road, Ealing, returned to find their cars had been hoisted up while workmen painted yellow lines on the road. Parking fine tickets were then attached to windscreens. Ealing Council backed down and cancelled the tickets after protests.

News of the World

A mother of three young children pulled over into a motorcycle parking bay in Cheam, Surrey, to help a child in the back seat who was choking. She was shocked when a parking attendant slapped a ticket on her windscreen. Sutton Council later said it was an 'unfortunate incident' and that they would reimburse the mother.

Guardian Society

In Kingston, Surrey, a traffic warden allowed an elderly couple to park momentarily on double yellow lines because her disabled husband needed assistance. A passing supervisor told the warden to give them a ticket. He refused and was sacked.

Guardian Society

Laura Helps returned to her car in Chatham to find the driver's window smashed and her CD collection stolen. She also found a parking fine notice for not displaying a pay and display ticket. Her valid ticket had blown off the dashboard and was lying among the broken glass. Medway Council apologised and revoked the fine.

Daily Mail

It was just a good old British tradition to the pensioners who went along to the Pier Hotel in Morecambe for a singalong every Monday. An organist from Blackpool played the popular tunes of yesteryear accompanied by a professional singer and the OAPs heartily gave voice in a music-hall style free and easy. But the local council said that the hotel needed an expensive entertainment licence if more than two people joined in the singing.

Morecambe Today* and *Daily Mail

In March 2005 a 400-yard stretch of Alum Rock Road in Saltley, Birmingham, was dubbed 'Britain's Most Warden Infested Street'. £334,000 was taken in parking fines in one year. The elderly, the sick and the disabled all got done and the milk deliveryman, who got six tickets, had a word for the local wardens: 'Ruthless'.

Divorce party, *see* page 76.

Chapter 18

Let Us Pray

Hopalong Chastity, the nun with a wooden leg...

These are statements about the Bible written by children in a school test:

- 'Lot's wife was a pillar of salt during the day, but a ball of fire during the night.'
- 'The seventh Commandment is thou shalt not admit adultery.'
- 'Jesus was born because Mary had an immaculate contraption.'
- 'St Paul preached holy acrimony.'
  'Christians have only one spouse. This is called monotony.' Duncan Mountford, Leatherhead, Surrey. *Daily Mail*

Billy Connolly, 61, got rave reviews when he returned to the London stage in September 2004. Bruce Dessau's review had the Big Yin revealing a friend who has developed a fat-free communion wine called 'I Can't Believe It's Not Jesus'.

Evening Standard

In the craze to distil great books into one paragraph comes this offering on the Bible: 'Good opening chapter. Main character arrives halfway through, but gets killed off early. Some decent Commandments. Cracking ending.'

Daily Telegraph

A notice board outside a church in Reading, close to a bus stop, carried the bold slogan: 'What will you be doing when the Day of Judgment comes?' Beneath it, this had been written: 'Still waiting for a Thames Valley bus.'

Edward Young, Reading, *The Times*

From a hymn sheet of St George's Parish Church, Chorley: 'Lead us to repeat our sins'. From the Eye Parish Newsletter: 'The meeting will be gin with prayer.'

Daily Telegraph

The Right Reverend Maxwell Homfray Maxwell-Gumbleton, Suffragan Bishop of Dunwich, Archdeacon of Sudbury and Rector of Hitcham in the 1930s, held that the best church committee consisted of himself as chairman, plus one member who never said anything and another who never turned up.

> David Turner, churchwarden, All Saints,
> Hitcham, Ipswich, *The Times*

A church pamphlet advised its Low Self Esteem Support Group to 'Please use the back door.'

> **J. Nutley, London SE7, *Daily Mail***

No one enjoyed the Cheltenham racing festival in March 2005 more than Canon Stephen Gregory, the racecourse chaplain. Canon Gregory, a self-confessed racing nut, said: 'What a heavenly job. I get to give the Sermon of the Mounts.'

> *Guardian*

'When looking for a Bible in a well-known chain of newsagents I found one at the bottom of the Humour section. Even better was the chain of cut-price booksellers who had Bibles on a 'Best Bargain' shelf.'

> **Geoffrey Hutchinson, Barnsley, South Yorkshire.**
> ***Daily Telegraph***

'I worked in a bookshop where I found a book on lacrosse in the religious section.'

> Michael Bentley, Bracknell, Berkshire.
> *Daily Telegraph*

187

A Bill which would make it illegal to tell religious jokes had its second reading in the House of Commons in December 2004, and the *Sun* ran a column of gags 'which the PC Brigade claim may cause offence'. They included:

- A man dies and goes to Heaven and asks the Virgin Mary why in all the paintings, sculptures, frescoes and carvings does she always look so sad. Mary looks around to see if anyone else is listening and says: 'To tell you the truth, I always wanted a girl.'

- Two priests go to Ibiza and decide to wear nothing which will identify them as clergymen. They are sitting in the sun in Hawaiian shirts, shorts and shades when a gorgeous blonde in a bikini greets them with: 'Good morning, Fathers.' 'How on earth did you know we are men of the cloth?' they asked. The shapely blonde replies: 'Fathers – it's me, Sister Helen.' *Sun*

A former Archbishop of Canterbury was asked by a New York reporter: 'Will you be visiting any night clubs while in New York?' The distinguished cleric replied: 'Are there any night clubs in New York?' A tabloid headline next day read: 'Archbishop asks if there are any night clubs in New York'.
David Hide, Malmesbury, Wiltshire. *Daily Telegraph*

When he was a young priest, Father Colin Myles Wilson, of Runcorn, Cheshire, visited an elderly gentleman in hospital and admired an elaborate coat of arms tattooed on the patient's chest. The man then leaped to his feet, dropped his pants to the floor in full view of the ward, and revealed, down the full length of his left leg, a tattoo of King Billy. On the other leg was Queen Mary. The man then brought his legs together – and the royal couple kissed.

Daily Telegraph

Irish comedian Dave Allen died in March 2005, aged 68. He was a raconteur who skewered the absurdities of authority, the Church and the Irish – often in notoriously ripe language. One of the jokes that offended the Mary Whitehouses and caused questions to be raised in the House of Commons was: 'We spend our lives by the clock. We get up by the clock, go to work by the clock, eat and sleep by the clock. Then we retire and what do they give us? A f*****g clock.'

The Times

Allen was taught by nuns and told this story about punishment from a mother superior. She'd say 'Do you want to be hit on the open hand or on the knuckles?' You'd say the open hand and she'd say: 'You've chosen the easy option. You must never do that. As you have chosen the easy way I'm going to hit you on the knuckles.' But if you chose the knuckles she would hit you on the knuckles.

The Times

On same day of its obituary on Allen, *The Times* published a report on religious humour by Rabbi Dr Jonathan Romain, minister of Maidenhead Synagogue. 'My God can survive jokes,' he said. 'It is not often appreciated what a strong role humour plays in religion, starting with the Bible.' The rabbi then told these two jokes:

- What do you call a nun with a wooden leg? Hopalong Chastity.'
- Who were the three constipated men in the Bible? Cain, who was not Abel. Moses, who took the tablets. Solomon who sat for 40 years.'

The Times published a list of '100 Things To Do This Easter' and was taken to task by reader Chris Walker, of Farnham, Surrey: 'Apparently, attending a church service is not one of them'.

The Times

Chapter 19

Media Madness

**Using a laptop may heat your testicles
and cause infertility...**

Bernard Levin's way of dealing with irritating
correspondents was a reply saying: 'I felt I should let
you know that an unregistered lunatic has obtained a
supply of your notepaper.' (Sir David Frost at Levin's
memorial service in October 2004).

The Times

When Richard Wallace was appointed editor of the
Daily Mirror in June 2004, he received a letter from
Kelvin MacKenzie, the swashbuckling former
editor of the *Sun*. 'Dear Richard Wallace, Just
checking if you are the same Richard Wallace who

was a drunken, idle, piss-poor showbiz reporter when I was editor of the *Sun*.'

Wallace responded: 'Dear Kelvin MacKenzie, Yes. Richard Wallace.'

Press Gazette

'Lie detector plan worries Cabinet'.

Headline in the *Guardian*

When Piers Morgan, the former editor of the *Daily Mirror*, told Cherie Blair that he had been sacked from the top job at the *Mirror*, the Prime Minister's wife exclaimed gleefully: 'Yes, we're still celebrating.'

Observer

Two quotes reported by the *Sun's* TV critic, Ally Ross:

- 'Manchester City's back four are playing like the Three Stooges.'
- On Channel 4's *Book Awards* programme David Suchet was asked: 'If you had to write an autobiography... who would it be about?'

Eighty per cent of newspaper readers do not read 'body copy' and rely on headlines, wrote Mark Daniel in the *Western Morning News*. They therefore live in a surreal world he said – and recalled some of his favourite headlines:

- Miners refuse to work after death
- Grandmother of eight makes hole in one
- High school drop-outs cut in half
- Juvenile court to try shooting defendant
- Milk drinkers turn to powder

Former *Daily Telegraph* editor Sir Max Hastings has been chosen for the Anthony Powell Society's Widmerpool award (presented to the public figure who most embodies the traits of Kenneth Widmerpool, a character in Powell's *A Dance to the Music of Time*). The Society's newsletter reminds readers that 'Widmerpool is variously pompous, self-obsessed and self-important; obsequious to those in authority and a bully to those below him.'

Independent

Attention all men – using a laptop may heat your testicles and cause infertility. *Guardian* headline. *The Times* version of this story was the second most-read item on www.timesonline.co.uk from 6 to 9 December 2004.

In March 2005, the *Sun* took delight in reporting that when the *Daily Express* picture library was asked for a photograph of Adolf Hitler, they responded with: 'Oh no, what's he done now?'

Sun

Dog swimming pool, *see* page 98.

Chapter 20

Food For Thought

Spotted Dick puts the wind up Americans...

As contestants in *I'm a Celebrity Get Me Out of Here* were eating maggots and other creepy crawlies, Michael Freeman, a photographer who took the pictures for a book called *Extreme Cuisine* (by Jerry Hopkins), said that he had eaten everything he photographed because 'a boyhood spent eating filthy food at English boarding schools had trained his palate to accept the impossible.'
Daily Telegraph

The fashionable restaurant of celebrity chef Jamie Oliver offers an upmarket version of beans on toast for £7. The *Guardian's* food editor Matthew Fort said baked beans were a healthy and nutritious dish – with an undesirable side effect: flatulence. He reminded readers that St Jerome told nuns in his charge to eschew beans in any form because 'they titillate the genitals'.

Fifty items of royal silver ware – ranging from giant, shell-shaped soup tureens to a 6ft candelabrum – went on public view at Windsor Castle in 2004. In 1844 the tureens were used by Queen Victoria to serve the Russian emperor 53 dishes, which included turtle soup and pureed cockerel's testicles.

Independent

Testicles managed to get into a more modern recipe in the *Game Cookbook* by Clarissa Dickson Wright, published in July 2004. Clarissa – one of the *Two Fat Ladies* in TV's cookery series – is also a Countryside Campaigner and her recipe for sautéed deer testicles was seen as a protest against the government's rural policies. She named the dish 'B******s to Blair'.

Sunday Times

A nation mourns. The makers of Bovril announce that in the wake of the BSE scare the quintessentially British beef drink will no longer have any beef in it. Yeast abstract is to be substituted. One angry chef said: 'It's like going to the butcher for a joint of beef and being offered a nut cutlet.'

Glasgow Evening Times/Daily Mail

The Michelin-starred restaurant Zafferano in Knightsbridge paid £28,000 in a charity auction for a giant Italian truffle. The media was invited to gaze upon and to sniff at the expensive (£600 a slice) delicacy – but not to taste it. Alan Hamilton sniffed and then wrote: 'There were subtle undertones of diesel, farmyard slurry... Brazil nuts, mushrooms and that kitchen cupboard we never got round to cleaning out last year.'

The Times

Following the Italian truffle, the French sent their smelliest cheeses to London in a contest which was won by Vieux Boulogne, a cow's milk cheese 7–9 weeks old. The *Guardian* reported that the prize-winner sent an aroma of six-week old earwax floating through the newspaper's offices... emitting a pleasant *eau de farmyard*, replete with dung and Barbour jackets. But 'behind the stinking rind' was a smooth cheese crying out for a jug of beer.

The *Independent's* report on the smelly cheese competition said of the winner: 'To the uninitiated it smells like the product of a cow's behind rather than its udders.'

***Guardian* diarist Simon Hoggart has been recording some of his readers' family sayings and loves the way they pass into family lore – making everyone laugh**

every time they are used. Among them is one from Catherine Moss, of Horsham, Sussex. She recalls the time a family friend came round for tea and, when offered a second helping of cake, replied: 'Just a small piece, like you gave me last time.' This became the standard family response to any offer of seconds.

Another comes from a Huddersfield woman whose ageing mother's cooking had begun to deteriorate. She produced an obviously over-cooked joint with the phrase: 'It's not as brown as it looks.'

Guardian

New Yorkers are still struggling to come to terms with many traditional British dishes. UK chefs in NY report that spotted dick and toad-in-the-hole 'frighten the life out of most Americans'. Some ask: 'Is there really a toad cooked in that hole?'. Others order spotted dick so that they can snigger. But they like fish and chips – probably 'because when they have them in Britain they are often drunk and it's usually the best thing they have ever eaten.'

Daily Telegraph

McDonald's announced that it is to give away pedometers with adult versions of its Happy Meals as part of a campaign to shake up the company's image as providers of unhealthy, high-fat, high-sugar food and encourage its customers to take more exercise. The *Daily Telegraph* pointed out that to burn off a Big Mac, large fries, large cola and McFlurry ice cream with Smarties (1,458 calories) would need a walk lasting five hours and 42 minutes.

Huntley & Palmers' biscuit tins were famously decorated with genteel, Edwardian-style paintings of idyllic English scenes. But, it has been discovered, artist Mick Hill enjoyed spicing them up with 'hidden' images such as copulating dogs and lovers having sex in a herbaceous border. They went unnoticed for years – but are now becoming collectors' items. 'I've always been a bit of a naughty boy,' says Mr Hill.

Mail on Sunday

One of these Huntley & Palmer biscuit tins came up for auction in 2004. At first glance it appears to show a sedate Edwardian garden party, but a closer inspection reveals that the mischievous artist had included a pair of copulating terriers, two naked lovers in and the word 'shit' on the side of a jam jar. The tin fetched £360.

Guardian

There were gasps of surprise at the Battisford Cricket Club in Suffolk when kitchen goddess Delia Smith admitted cheating. The queen of British cookery used to be lavishly praised for the teas she prepared for her husband's village cricket team. But when she formally opened the club's new pavilion she confessed that sometimes she would 'get sandwiches from Marks and Spencer'.

David Sapsted, *Daily Telegraph*

Friar Tuck was not alone. Research has shown that Robin Hood's rotund monk had hundreds of real-life medieval counterparts. They wolfed down suet, lard and butter in 'startling quantities' – taking in about 6,000 calories a day and even 4,500 when they were fasting.

Guardian

Prince Charles thought the fruitcake baked by grandmother Etta Richardson, 74, from the village of Llansteffan, near Carmarthen, was the best he had ever tasted. But she refused to let him have the recipe. It was an old family treasure handed down from generation to generation, she said, and had never been written down.

The Times

A local councillor who weighs 19 stone has launched a campaign against unhealthy eating. She insists she is ideal for the job because she is a prime example of Britain's alarming rates of obesity. She is Councillor Diane Inch of Halton Borough, Cheshire.

Daily Star

In August 2004 the Ministry of Defence released details of the new ration packs to be provided for

British soldiers. Bully beef was out, chicken madras and spicy sauces were in. *The Times* emphasised how important good food was for an army marching on its stomach and recalled that, when returning from battle, the Duke of Wellington spotted the white cliffs of Dover and was heard to cry: 'Buttered toast, buttered toast.'

At my grammar school in the 1950s we had domestic science lessons. I remember being given the ingredients for 'cauliflower au gratin' which included margarine and white bread. The cauliflower had to be boiled for 40 minutes. My French mother denounced this barbarity and I was excused domestic science as I had a difficult foreign mother. The English continued in their unreformed way without challenge.

Jane Lawson, London, *Independent*

As we tuck in to more and more to foreign dishes it is predicted that shepherd's pie, fish and chips and roast dinners will disappear from our menus within a generation. The only traditional British dish likely to survive is bangers and mash, say researchers from Sainsbury. 4Meanwhile, start looking forward to pomegranate squash, moonfish fingers, quinoa (a low-carb potato substitute from Peru) and hiziki (a highly flavoured sea plant).

Daily Express/ The Times

There is praise for Penny Holmes, the wife of the British ambassador to Paris, who has written a cookbook in French designed to show that contemporary English food rises above boiled cabbage and mutton. The *Guardian's* coverage of this unique book event reminded readers that the French are prone to dismiss British cooking with: 'If it's cold, it's soup. If it's warm it's beer.' It also said that the page devoted to 'Le meilleur pudding au monde' (Christmas pudding) was commendably brave, given that most French people look upon it with abject, nausea-infused horror – particularly as the recipe comes with a recommendation that the dish can be kept for several years.

Dozens of seats on the *Queen Mary II* are being broken under the weight of obese passengers. A spokesman said: 'We do have many large passengers. We have 10 restaurants, so if they are big when they get on, they tend to be bigger when they get off.' Many of the broken seats were in the bar and restaurant areas.

Sunday Telegraph

Financial adviser Jon Cofield, of Bromsgrove, Worcestershire, has had nothing else but bacon sandwiches as his main meal for 45 years. Every evening he has a sandwich with four rashers and brown sauce. 'I love butties,' he says. 'I had one for Christmas dinner –

with holly on top.' John, whose wife and two children eat normal meals, is 5ft 10ins and a slim 10st 6lb.

Sun

An e-mail doing the rounds on the Internet lists some of the quirkiest aspects of our daily lives:

- A pizza can get to your house faster than an ambulance.
- People order double cheeseburgers, large fries and DIET coke.
- Shops sell lemon juice made with artificial flavour and dishwashing liquid made with real lemons. *Sun*

A Guildford couple who pointed out to their local Tesco that their bread rolls were on sale for 15p each or six for £1 *were* disappointed to see the prices adjusted to 19p each or six for £1.

Daily Mail

It was reported as the biggest food scare ever – the fact that a chilli powder called Sudan 1, used in hundreds of products, might possibly trigger cancer. In the midst of the panic the *Sunday Telegraph* told of a chemist called Arthur Hassell who used the *Lancet* medical journal to name and shame shops selling fraudulent products – including pickled vegetables dyed green with copper. No panic, though – Mr Hassell was writing in the Lancet of the 1850s.

The *Sunday Telegraph* also commented that many consumers assume that modern food is much less pure than in earlier times. But in the 1850s not a single shop in London was selling mustard in an unadulterated form, children's sweets were dyed with lead and copper-based colours and bread was routinely whitened with alum. Cayenne was frequently coloured with highly toxic red lead or lead oxide. Compared with this, Sudan 1 is relatively harmless. *Sunday Telegraph* headline: 'These scares are one of the Great British Traditions'.

The campaign by chef Jamie Oliver to improve school meals reminded Geoff Wright, of Doncaster, of the rhyme dedicated to school menus in his part of South Yorkshire:

Dead dogs' giblets
Green cats' eyes
All mixed together with a snot and bogie pie
Horses' skin all green and thick
All washed down with a cup of cold sick
Daily Telegraph

Chapter 21

Royal Flush

Charles is a rat and Camilla is a pig...

When asked what his favourite opera was, King George V replied: '*La Bohème*. It's the shortest.'

Daily Telegraph

Amid stories that churchgoers are failing to put enough cash on the offertory plate, it was reported that the Queen's staff iron a £5 note ready for her church collection each Sunday.

The Times

It is said that the Queen uses her handbag to send silent messages to her staff. If it is dangling loosely from her left arm, then all is well. But if she switches the bag to

her right arm, it's a signal that she is bored with the person she is with and needs to be rescued.

Daily Mail

The Queen and Prince Philip were attending a Royal Variety Performance and Elton John was top of the bill – with his back to the royal box.

'I wish,' said the Queen, 'he would turn the microphone to one side.'

'I wish,' said Philip, 'he would turn the microphone off.' From Gyles Brandreth's book, *Philip & Elizabeth: Portrait of a Marriage.*

Sunday Telegraph

After a man breached royal security by climbing onto a Buckingham Palace balcony in a Batman outfit, Michael Holmes of Liverpool wrote to the *Guardian*: 'A person in a silly costume appears and waves to the crowd below. Nothing new there, then.'

Yorkshireman Charles Haslett earns a crust as a Prince Charles look-a-like and the *Daily Mail* reported that he boasts a royal-shaped nose and bottom – 'meaning an oversized conk, wide hips and short legs'.

Three workmen who got lost on the Windsor Estate asked for directions from a pensioner out walking her dogs. As the lady began giving directions the workmen realised the dogs were corgis and that the person they had stopped was the Queen. Cheekily they asked Her Majesty for her autograph. Unfazed she replied jokingly: 'Sorry, one doesn't do autographs.'

News of the World

In 1996 the Queen was reportedly 'very unimpressed' with a portrait by Anthony Williams which some thought made her look 20 years too old. One critic said that it made Her Majesty look like 'an OAP about to lose her bungalow'.

The Times

A portrait of Queen Elizabeth II, commissioned to mark the 800th year of Jersey's allegiance to the throne, cost £150,000. Her reported opinion of it was: 'It makes me look like an old woman lost in a wood.'

Daily Telegraph

Stuart Pearson Wright's portrait of Prince Philip shows him with an elongated face, a big nose, a hairy bare chest, a bluebottle on his naked shoulder and mustard cress growing on his right forefinger. 'Gadzooks!' said the Duke of Edinburgh. 'Why have you given me such a great schonk?'

Asked by the artist if he thought the portrait resembled him, the Prince said: 'I bloody well hope not.'

Daily Telegraph, Times, Guardian, Evening Standard (and practically every other newspaper)

For his stay in a spartan Greek monastery on Mount Athos – where the monks sleep in bare cells and dine off bean stew – Prince Charles took with him 30 suitcases, a special cushion for his back, a satellite phone and his own tuck box.

Daily Mail

'The Prince of Wales breakfasts off wheatgerm, lunches off dry bread and dines like the Emperor Nero… His grandfather used to kick furniture so hard that his hosts hid their antiques when he came to stay… A former servant claims that Charles wrenched a hand basin from the wall and wrote terse notes to staff: "This sponge is dry. Please see that it is watered immediately… Camilla is a jolly Gloucestershire matron with a voice that could trigger a Klosters avalanche."

From a page long profile in the
Observer of 3 April 2005

Among the Gloucestershire set, Camilla is known as 'a bit of all right' – earthy fun and just what the doctor ordered.
Observer, 10 April 2005

The day after it was announced that Prince Charles and Camilla were to marry (11 February 2005), *The Times* carried a page-one story saying: 'He is a rat and she is a pig and this means that they are compatible'. The article was referring to their animal signs determined by dates of birth under Chinese astrology.

The Times

The regional paper that covers the area where Prince Charles has his Gloucestershire home knew how to handle a big story. 'Tetbury Man to Wed' was the splash headline in the *Bristol Evening Post*.

Sunday Times

It is said that when Camilla first met Charles some 30 years ago the first words she said to him were: 'My great-grandmother and your great-great grandfather were lovers. So how about it?'

Guardian and many other papers around the world

According to biographer Rebecca Tyrrel, school friends remembered Camilla bragging about her illustrious ancestor, the official mistress of King Edward VII, who said: 'My job is to curtsey first and then jump into bed.'

Guardian

Allison Pearson wrote of 'an England within England, a complaisant sliver of society that until recently conducted its affairs much as it did when the great country houses had name plates on the bedroom doors to guide nocturnal adulterers.'

Sunday Times

Allison Pearson also writes that Camilla once asked Charles for a copy of a speech he had just made... 'Greater love hath no woman than to lay down an afternoon for a tract on Business in the Community.'

Sunday Times

Elizabeth Grice reported that shortly before the wedding Diana told her two sisters that she wanted to call off the marriage. 'Bad luck,' they are alleged to have joshed. 'Your face is on the tea towels so you're too late to chicken out.'

Daily Telegraph

Within hours of the wedding date being announced some hotel rooms in Windsor went up from around £190 a night to £2,000 for the occasion.

Daily Telegraph

When Prince Charles married Camilla, British newspapers ranged from the effusive to the vulgar. The *Daily Express* had an edition that carried the story on pages 1, 2, 3, 4, 5, 6, 7, 8, 9, 10, 11, 24 and 25. The *Independent* pointedly filled its front page with non-royal-wedding news, and the *Star* carried the headline 'Boring Old Gits To Wed' – (combined ages 113).

Press Gazette

Coverage of the romance of Prince Charles and Camilla was not restricted to British newspapers, but the international press were not always very kind. When it was reported that the Queen would not be attending the wedding at Windsor's town hall the *New York Post* headline was: 'Queen to skip Chuck nups'.

Daily Telegraph

The annual turnover of the royal memorabilia industry is reportedly around £10 million. It swung into action quickly after Charles and Camilla got engaged.

- Asda offered a £19 replica of the engagement ring. The original is thought to be worth about £500,000.
- A website offered a 'Charles and Diana Mug Conversion' guide which advised putting a Camilla sticker over Diana's face.
- Postcard vendors in Windsor were reported to be slashing the prices of cards featuring Diana.
- A woman in South Norwood, London, did a brisk trade in Charles and Camilla badges and fridge magnets, which she makes at home. 'I have no idea why anybody would want to buy this stuff, ' she said. 'But I am not complaining.'
Sunday Telegraph

After the wedding of Prince Charles and Camilla on 9 April 2005, the Queen hosted a reception at Windsor Castle. She told 800 guests she had two important announcements to make. The first was that Hedgehunter had won the Grand National. Then she welcomed Charles and his bride to the 'Winners Enclosure'. 'They have overcome Becher's Brook and all kinds of other terrible obstacles... and my son is home and dry with the woman he loves.'

Sunday Telegraph

A couple of days before the royal wedding in Windsor registrar's office, a *Sun* reporter drove a van through the gates of Windsor Castle and claimed he could have exploded a bomb there. Next day (8 April 2005) papers ranging from the *Times* to the *Sun* published a photograph of police at the Castle positioning a notice which read: 'SLOW POLICE'.

The Queen Mother's bedroom at the Castle of Mey, her former summer retreat in Caithness, Scotland, was opened to the public for the first time in May 2004. The *Daily Mail* reported: 'It owes more to three-star B&B than royal opulence... Visitors will see a copy of *Hello!* magazine on the bedside table. The *Racing Post* will not be in evidence.' A guest bathroom at the Castle is described as 'austere'.

Princess Michael of Kent – whose husband is the Queen's first cousin – is often referred to in the press as 'Princess Pushy'. *The Times* quoted her as once having said: 'I have a better background than anyone else who's married into the Royal Family since the war, excepting Prince Philip.' The following quote on the Princess is attributed to the Queen: 'Far too grand for the likes of us.'

The Times

Asked if loo rolls should be wound under or over a dispenser, former royal servant Paul Burrell replied: 'Over. If it were down they would unravel. But Royals don't have that problem. Instead they have tissues which are fanned out into an attractive display and sit in a box.'

Independent

In a collection of his essays *Brief Lives*, W.F. Deedes tells of Princess Diana's phobia about the long lenses of photographers. 'When Prince William was young, she discussed her fears with one or two of us and asked how it would be if, while out with his nanny in the park, he was taken short and photographed relieving himself behind a tree? That struck us as far fetched but not long after, he was photographed having a pee behind a tree and the picture appeared in a German magazine.'

Daily Telegraph

An entrepreneur has come up with the idea of marketing Diana and Dodi dolls 'just like Barbie and Ken'. The idea horrified the Diana, Princess of Wales Memorial Fund which has already had to fight off attempts to produce Diana lavatory seat covers, comics, sporting goods, condoms, sunglasses, matches, candles and colonic irrigation kits.

The Times

The late Queen Mother's wartime ration book is now part of the official Royal Collection. The Royals did take rationing seriously and a dinner in honour of Eleanor Roosevelt at Buckingham Palace in 1942 included fish cakes, cold ham, chicken and Brussels sprouts. Said a Royal source: 'It was not luxurious food, but it was served on gold and silver plates.'

Daily Mail

Prince Charles' organic carrots, grown at Home Farm, Gloucestershire, were rejected by supermarkets because they were too crooked. Then they turned down his potatoes because they were not shiny enough. Farm manager David Wilson blames major stores for wanting 'cosmetic perfection'. The prince's 'dull' and 'crooked' veg now go to local schools.

Daily Telegraph

Prince Charles rode in a London black cab on 20 July 2004 and driver John Sheen said: 'Six quid on the meter. He gives me a tenner and insists I keep the change. Diamond geezer.' Cabbies' chef Faye Olsson 'tries to tempt him with one of her fantastic bacon butties or a black pudding roll, only a quid each, but he says nah. Must have had his scoff before he came out.'

Alan Hamilton in *The Times*.

In a BBC documentary, chefs who have cooked for the Royal Family (including Gary Rhodes and Antony Worrall Thompson) revealed:

- The Queen likes her Martini stirred, not shaken.
- Her Sunday roast is recycled into cottage pies or rissoles.
- She dislikes spicy food and tomato pips because they get stuck in her teeth.

Worrall Thompson said that on the way to prepare a Royal lunch for 1,500 he was caught speeding, having overslept. The court let him off with just a couple of points on his licence after he argued that he had been forced to choose between the law and his Queen and country.

The Times

When it was announced that Prince Harry was to become an officer cadet at Sandhurst, the *Daily Telegraph's* cartoonist Matt drew two soldiers discussing the news. One of them is saying: 'All the hard drinking and boisterousness will be a shock, but I suppose we'll get used to it.' However, Prince Harry will have to submit to fierce discipline at Sandhurst, where drill instructors are known for showing no fear or favour to crowned heads and heirs to thrones. The future King of Jordan was once told: 'You're a horrible little man, Prince Hussein, sir.'

Daily Telegraph

Channel 4 received many complaints when it moved the *Countdown* quiz show from its 4.30pm slot to 3.15pm. Tim Walker in the *Sunday Telegraph* writes that 'although it would be a constitutional monstrosity for the Queen to write to a TV station, I am informed that she, too, dislikes the new timing... because it clashes with her afternoon walk with the corgis.'

A few days after Prince William made the front pages with an early morning fracas outside a London night club, his father was the subject of a shock *Daily Telegraph* headline: 'Charles almost ends up with a Turkish wife.' He was visiting the 7,000-year-old stone city of Mardin, by the Mesopotamian plain, when he was served a cup of coffee from the tray of 26-year-old Berna Yagci. He enjoyed the coffee and was about to put the cup back on the tray when an official warned him that the coffee ceremony is a local tradition in which the beverage is offered by potential wives. If the man places the cup back onto the woman's tray then he is betrothed to the one who served him. Afterwards Berna, who is not married and does not have a boyfriend, joked: 'I nearly became a princess.'

Princess Alice, Duchess of Gloucester, died aged 102 in October 2004. Her former butler Peter Russell remembered how she and her husband used to dine alone at a 22ft mahogany table laden with silver candlesticks and model soldiers down the middle. The Duke always dressed formally and sat at the head of table. The Duchess, who brought her knitting to each meal and did a few rows between courses, sat about four yards down on his right. He was hard of hearing, so she would ask Russell to pass on messages:

'Could you ask His Royal Highness if he knows what he is doing tomorrow?'

Butler pads to within Duke's hearing distance: 'Her Royal Highness would like to know if Your Royal Highness knows what he is doing tomorrow.'

Duke: ''Course I bloody don't. Nobody has bloody told me.'

Daily Mail

At the age of 83 Prince Philip was still astonishing spectators with his skill and daring in the hazardous sport of carriage driving. In 2004 he revealed some of his secrets in a book called *30 Years On and Off the Box Seat*. In winter he keeps warm with moleskin trousers plus padded Gore-tex over-trousers and 'moon-boots' from China. 'After years of trial I wear one pair of gloves under a second pair of heavy pigskin gloves. I then came across some electrically heated under-gloves. You strap a pair of batteries above the wrists and plug them into heating elements that cover the backs of the hands and fingers... To top it off I wear a deerstalker hat... I may look like Inspector Clouseau in pursuit of the Pink Panther in the Arctic, but it is effective.'

Daily Telegraph

The Queen sees to the feeding of her corgis whenever she can. The dogs' food is sent up in a dumb waiter and is handed to Her Majesty by a footman. On the floor on a tablecloth stand individual bowls with the dog's names on them. Wearing rubber gloves, the Queen mixes meat, vegetables, gravy and biscuits and when the corgis have finished she clears things up and returns the bowls to a tray.

From *The Queen, Rupert & Me*, by Australian journalist and author Desmond Zwar, who wrote the story for the *Daily Mail*.

On the day the Queen wore her glittering crown to make the Queen's Speech in Westminster in November 2004, former royal butler Paul Burrell claimed he had once seen her wearing the crown on her head and pink, fluffy slippers on her feet. She was practising wearing it for the Opening of Parliament.

Sun

When Prince Charles sits working at his desk, the royal posterior is comfortable on the plumped-up cushion that is carried around for him to use wherever he goes. Charles tries to stick to food cooked by his own staff, who know that his vegetables may only be steamed in a particular brand of mineral water.

Independent on Sunday

Prince Charles was a cellist in his youth and is one of the few people on the planet to employ a personal harpist.

Guardian

Newspapers worldwide attacked Prince Harry for turning up at a party dressed as a swastika-wearing Nazi. But *The Times* found room on page one to let another 20-year-old say: 'It just reaffirms that he is as stupid as everyone else our age.'

When an embarrassed guest's mobile phone rang in the Queen's presence she gently advised: 'You had better answer that. It might be somebody important.'

Daily Mirror

Prince Andrew was taken to task for making too many expensive helicopter trips instead of using public transport. A former senior railway employee reminded him that when a member of the Royal family travels on a regular train:

- The coaches that would have formed that train will be swapped for some just out of maintenance.
- They will be externally cleaned.
- On-train cleaners will travel on the inward journey.
- A traction inspector will ride with the driver.
- A travelling fitter (engineer) will ride the train.
- The signaller will be advised, to ensure that the train has a clear run.

'All that for £97 – not bad', says Chris Hales of Hertfordshire.

Daily Telegraph

During a Royal campaign to economise the Duke of Edinburgh was urged to switch off the lights when leaving a room. He was apparently heard to complain that he would next be forced to travel on a pensioner's bus pass.

Guardian

Prince Charles said to one of his former advisers: 'I can't see the point of employing advisers who disagree with me.'

Harry Mount's Notebook, *Daily Telegraph*

Jan McGerk, reporting from Bangkok, writes 'Queen Victoria strikes me as a rather prim sex deity in this city known for its steamy nights.' But a rather frumpy statue of her in the British Embassy has become a fertility rite for Bangkok's childless. 'Fresh garlands are regularly placed on the regal bronze lap... and new parents drop off posies in thanks when babies are born.'

Independent on Sunday

Coughing Parrot, *see* page 103.

Chapter 22

Mind Your Language

**Where does the Scottish accent stop
and the English one start?**

**Eight-year-old Tanmay Dixit of Manchester became the
youngest winner on the TV game show *Countdown*. His
winning words included FANNIES and FARTED which
had others on the show roaring with laughter.**

Sun

When searching for herbs in a supermarket, Ken
Evans of Saltford, Somerset, asked a young
assistant: 'Do you sell cloves?' The assistant
replied: 'Only T-shirts'.

Daily Telegraph

Puns are often said to be the lowest form of wit – but Philip Howard points out that some 3,000 puns have been found in Shakespeare's plays.

The Times

Yellow Pages hunted down some of the punniest business names:

- The Vinyl Resting Place – a record shop in Croydon.
- A Fish Called Rhondda – a fish and chip shop in Wales.
- Melon Cauli – a greengrocer in Birmingham.
- Poultry in Motion – a poultry housing specialist in Norfolk.
- Jim'll Mix It – a concrete firm in East London.
- Crease Lightning – an ironing service in Bristol. *Daily Mail*

A *Daily Telegraph* reader wrote in to thank its crossword compiler for the realisation that 'Aha, Prescott' is an anagram of 'catastrophe'.

Following an article in the *Independent* about the 'chaotic English language', David Courtney of Dover reminds us of a sentence to test foreigners (using 'ough' pronounced in several different ways): 'The dough-faced, ploughboy, coughed and hiccoughed his way through Loughborough.'

Independent

This was followed by a letter from Jonathan Pickering, of Farnham, Surrey with: 'The rough-coated, dough-faced ploughman, wandered thoughtfully, coughing and hiccoughing through the streets of Scarborough on his way to the loughs of Ireland... Ough in nine different renditions.'

Independent

The ever-evolving English language is renowned for adopting new words from every conceivable source. The words 'arsed', 'bumfluff', 'shagtastic' and 'sparrowfart' have achieved a new level of respectability, graduating from schoolroom indecency to recognition on the Scrabble board. They are included among 45,000 new words in the 2004 edition of *Collins Scrabble Words*.

The Times

The Queen is a Scrabble fan.

Sun

English is also the villain behind the quip about the UK and the USA being two nations divided by a single language. Example in *The Times*: When an American visited C.S. Lewis in Oxford the author fed him three pots of tea. After the third pot the visitor asked for the bathroom. Lewis courteously led him into a room containing only a bath and produced some towels and a bar of soap.

Shakespeare's most famous quotations are less well known than the sayings of David Brent, the fictional middle-manager from the BBC TV series *The Office*, according to a survey. Brent's comment: 'Remember that age and treachery will always triumph over youth and ability' was recognised by more 25-to-44-year-olds than 'Brevity is the soul of wit' from *Hamlet*. Other findings by the survey included:

- A third of those questioned remembered Brent's 'Accept that some days you are the pigeon and some days you are the statue' but only ten per cent knew that 'Now is the winter of our discontent' is from *Richard III*.
- Some thought that in Shakespeare's *Julius Caesar*, 'Friends, Romans and countrymen' were asked to lend money or their swords rather than their ears.
- Other literary blunders came from those asked to complete the opening line of Wordsworth's *Daffodils*: 'I wandered lonely as a *****'. Answers included: 'bear, sheep, pigeon, tree and goat.' *Daily Telegraph*

In a leader on tipping, *The Times* said the word may come from 18th-century England, where cafes used to feature a little box by the door with 'To Insure Promptitude' written on the side.

Carlisle's tourist information office was asked by a traveller to show him on a map where the Scottish accent stops and the English one starts.

Sunday Times

It turned out not be such a daft question after *The Times* later reported that the border town of Berwick-upon-Tweed, after 600 years of doubtful nationality, had apparently decided to be English, not Scottish. Berwick's unique blend of Scottish and northern English is gradually being replaced by a more pronounced English accent. They used to say 'barry' for good and 'joogle' for dog, but those Scots dialect words are now rarely heard. Berwick's football team still plays in the Scottish League and legend has it that the town is still technically at war with Russia. The declaration of hostilities in the Crimea in 1854 was made in the name of Great Britain, Ireland and Berwick. But the town's name got left off the subsequent peace treaty.

The Times

Lynn Truss, author of the best selling book on punctuation (*Eats, Shoots and Leaves*), is also a stickler about the proper use of words. She tells how the driver of a car she was travelling in offered to stop at a newsagent's. 'But as he slowed, I said: "No, look it says 'stationary' with an A; we'll go somewhere else." He laughed politely, but I wasn't joking.'

Daily Telegraph

The Plain English Campaign marked its 25th anniversary by nominating their choicest item of gobbledegook. It came from the 1998 National Minimum Wage Regulations and said: 'The hours of non-hours worked by a worker in a pay reference period shall be the total of the number of hours spent by him during the pay reference period in carrying out the duties required of him under his contract to do non-hours work.'

Guardian

Michael Williams, Readers' Editor of the *Independent on Sunday* reports that 'independent' is one of the most frequently misspelled words in English. The most commonly misspelled words (in descending order) are: weird, definitely, ecstasy, accidentally, occurrence, cemetery, liaison and peddler.

Independent on Sunday

Williams advises the use of dictionaries rather than computer spellchecks and says: 'Never rely on pronunciation and pity the foreigner, as this little rhyme demonstrates:

> "A young man called Cholmondeley Colqhoun
> Kept as a pet a babolquhoun
> His mother said: 'Cholmondeley,
> Do you think it colmondeley
> To feed you babolquhoun with a spolquhoun?'"
> *Independent on Sunday*

All official documents in the Vatican are still written in Latin – but some modern words have wormed their way into the lexicon:

- Hot pants have become *brevissimae bracae femineae.*
- Punk – *punkianae catervae assecla.*
- Pub – *publica potoria taberna.*
- Playboy – *juvenis voluptarius.*
- Night Club – *taberna nocturna.*
  Sunday Telegraph

The group of Austrian GPs recruited to work in South Yorkshire all spoke perfect English. But this was not always enough to cope with the dialects of folk from places like Barnsley and Doncaster. Among the terms that baffled the new GPs were tuppence, Uncle Sam, chip, thingy, tail, sixpence, floo, doofer, sparrow and widgy – all of which refer to male or female sex organs. They also had to get used to patients complaining of 'feeling jiggered'.

Guardian/Daily Telegraph

Chapter 23

Golden Oldies

**Man reserves sun beds by placing his toupee
and dentures on them. They were both stolen...**

'Sorry to keep you,' said a lady who took a long time to answer the door. 'I've been gardening and I feel tired. I must expect it, I suppose – I am 91. Oh, how I wish I could be 80 again.'

Ronald Chatwin, Hellingly, East Sussex, *The Times*

When he was 93, George Burney was asked what sex was like. His reply: "Like playing billiards with a rope".

From John Murray's *A Gentleman Publisher's Commonplace Book*, quoted in Andrew Marr's column in the *Daily Telegraph*

Eastbourne is tired of the old joke: 'Dover for the Continent, Eastbourne for the incontinent'. Also for being known as God's Waiting Room. The resort is attempting to attract younger visitors by introducing 'double-width deck chairs designed for amorous couples.'

David Sapsted, *Daily Telegraph*

The Times crossword celebrated its 75th birthday on 1 February 2005. The paper's crossword editor, Richard Browne, told how he treasured this letter from an elderly lady: 'I always do the crossword first thing in the morning to see if I have enough marbles left to make it worth my while getting up.'

The Times

An 87-year-old woman who hosted all-night parties in her sheltered housing flat was allowed to carry on living there provided she changed her life style. Grimsby Crown Court heard that the lady's front room in Beverley, East Yorkshire, was dubbed 'more a saloon bar than a sitting room'. She promised to settle for a quieter routine.

Guardian

A cousin of Tim Matthew from Wells-next-the-Sea has received a letter from the social services asking if she has considered applying for a job seeker's allowance. His cousin is 101 years old.

Daily Telegraph

The Prudential has come up with a new word to describe modern old folk who are turning their backs on bingo and knitting and going for much livelier pastimes: 'Geri-actives'.

The Times

Grandmother Mary Limond, 75, admitted driving carelessly at speeds between 5mph and 35mph, causing a huge traffic queue. She was fined £200 and had six points added to her licence at Stirling Sheriff Court. She said that new glasses left her dazzled by oncoming cars.

Daily Telegraph

A notice in Bridlington's WRVS office asked volunteers to let them know when they reached 75. 'Head Office are collating statistics,' it said, 'and need to know how many volunteers (not broken down by age and sex) there are.' Mike Wilson, Bridlington, East Yorkshire.

Daily Mail

Lawrence and Dorothy Rigby, 75 and 82, have been holidaying at the same seaside hotel for 30 years. They have visited the Belmont in Sidmouth, Devon, 220 times.

Daily Express

The *Express* story on Lawrence and Dorothy included a glimpse of life in Sidmouth, reminding readers that the resort is home to almost three quarters of the UK's donkeys and that in 1819 Queen Victoria was nearly hit by a bird hunter's gunshot when visiting there.

Alf Meadows, 67, of Bury St Edmunds, Suffolk, reserved two sun beds at a holiday resort in Malta – by placing his toupee and dentures on them. They were both stolen.

Sun

Alan Thompson, 71, and his wife Yvonne, 68, of Oxton, Wirral, have bought the 'courting bench' where they fell in love 50 years ago.

Sun

A 100-year-old blind and deaf woman who lives on her own in Sheffield has been refused a place in a care home. She was told 'you are too fit'.

Daily Express

St Annes Conservative Club near Blackpool has a genteel reputation – a bastion of tradition and respectability. It has tea dances, an attentive doorman and portraits of the Queen, Margaret Thatcher and Winston Churchill. But after a tip-off, police uncovered a shoplifting ring run by two women members in their eighties. After an investigation the ladies

were arrested, given formal cautions – and barred from the club. Police spent three weeks unravelling the scandal – and called the inquiry 'Operation Bluerinse'.

The Times

Sidney Prior celebrated his 90th birthday in November 2004 – with his workmates at B&Q in Wimbledon. He gets up at 4am every day, cooks himself a full English breakfast and prepares a packed lunch before catching the Tube to work. He remembers his first job – earning 50p a week – and how 'We all had to wear trilbies and raise our hats whenever we saw a lady.'

Daily Mail

When Rosalind Strover was 90, her daughter-in-law Jennifer placed a 100–1 bet that the old lady would live to be 100. In November 2004 Rosalind clocked up her century and William Hill paid out £12,000. Every penny of the winnings went on a spectacular party for 200 family and friends in Mrs Strover's care home in Colchester.

Daily Mail

William Wagstaffe, 95, has given up his bicycle after riding it almost every day for 75 years. He spent his £14 life savings on the bike on 14 May 1929 and has worn out three saddles and 15 sets of tyres. He biked from his home in Croydon to work in

Bermondsey, London, and did so throughout the Blitz. The bicycle is now with the Transport Museum in London, complete with original saddle bag and tool kit – and an oil lamp still masked with blackout tape. Museum curator Robert Excell said: 'The bicycle is remarkably well preserved. They made them from stronger steel in those days.'

Daily Mirror

Two elderly men were served with Anti-Social Behaviour Orders for regularly inviting prostitutes to their sheltered accommodation in Birmingham.

Daily Telegraph

Chinaman Guo Cairo, aged 105, is to make a bid to become the world's fastest centenarian – running the 100 metres for 100-year-olds. He needs to beat 30.86 seconds, the time clocked up by the current champion, South African Philip Babinowitz of South Africa.

Independent on Sunday

Chapter 24

Just The Job

**By 1960 work will be limited to three hours a day...
(Forecast made in 1936)**

A financial adviser in Bedfordshire received a letter
from the Prudential offering to save him money
on his insurance. The letter began: 'Dear Mr
Shagslikeadonkey...'. The men from the Pru blamed a
prankster no longer in their employ.

Independent on Sunday

Many columns were filled with newspaper stories
about British workers taking too many 'sickies' –
particularly those in the public sector. Michael
Poole of Wraysbury, Berkshire, recalled that in the
1950s, when he worked for the Ministry of

Defence, a senior executive demanded to know why he had taken no sick leave. 'Because I haven't been sick,' he replied. 'What's that got to do with it?' was the response. 'Take a week off. You're making the rest of us look bad.'

The Times

A welter of stories about British workers taking too many days off work reminded David Brancher, of Monmouthshire, of advice given by an exasperated university vice chancellor: 'Never call a meeting for a Wednesday. You will find it cuts into two weekends.'

The Times

A video game store in Edinburgh advertised their latest games with 'Get your sick notes ready.'

Spotted by Clive Collins, Hadleigh,
Essex, *Daily Telegraph*

The BBC e-mailed its staff with details about its self-assertive training course. An earnest young man applied along with a note saying 'but I will need to clear it with my deputy manager first'.

Guardian

When Pauline Millican told a Liverpool job centre that she wanted to advertise for a hard-working receptionist for her family's opticians practice she was told: 'You can't use the phrase 'hard-working'. It's discriminatory.'

Mail on Sunday

A job centre in Hampshire rejected an advertisement seeking 'warehouse packers who must be hard-working' – claiming that it discriminated against those who were not.

Independent on Sunday

'By 1960, work will be limited to three hours a day.' A forecast made by John Langdon-Davies in *A Short History of the Future* (1936).

Reader's Digest

Those who own dishwashers, deep freezers, clothes dryers, microwaves and other 'time saving' devices can sometimes end up taking longer to do their chores than those who do not. University researchers reported that owning a clothes dryer can actually increase the amount of time spent on laundry by three minutes a day. People with lawnmowers and hedge trimmers spend about nine minutes longer a day looking after the garden.

Sunday Times/British Journal of Sociology

Research by the insurance firm Esure concluded that there are £3.1billion pounds' worth of unused domestic gadgets in British homes. Top of the list of unused appliances is the sandwich toaster, followed by electric knives, vegetable preparation devices, foot-spas, bread-makers, fondue sets and electric tin-openers.

Daily Mail

Tommy Cone, 65, quit his £4.50-an-hour security guard job when he won £4.2m on the lottery. Eighteen months later he asked for his job back at a shopping centre in Oldham, Lancashire – because he was bored.

Sun

Simon Burrell, 28, of Southampton, applied for a job as a postman, but changed his mind and got a job elsewhere. But the Royal Mail started sending him weekly pay cheques which added up to £1,530.56p before he finally got it through to them: 'I haven't done a single day's work for you.' (He also got a Royal Mail Christmas card, some holiday vouchers, 50 first-class stamps – and a message thanking him for 'another year of real progress.')

Sun

Chapter 25

Christmas Presence

Legless man gets socks for Christmas...

The best way to empty a bar at closing time is to put on a record by Cliff Richard, according to researchers who watched the reaction of drinkers to a variety of festive tunes. They discovered that Cliff's 1988 hit *Mistletoe and Wine* did the trick. A spokesman for John Barras pubs said: 'Christmas wouldn't be Christmas without Cliff. He certainly gets the customers to drink up.'
Sunday Times

Bill Clarke, of South Chailey, East Sussex, tells how he lets his daughter (who specialises in garden history) choose whatever she likes for Christmas. Her 2004 choice presented him with a problem in presentation and wrapping – she chose a lorry load of compost.

Daily Telegraph

At his sheltered accommodation in Manchester, Stan Coram got socks for Christmas – despite having no legs. He also got chocolates but couldn't eat them because he is diabetic. 'You have to laugh,' said Stan, 73.

Sunday Times

Simon Hoggart, writing about his book on yukky round-robin Christmas letters, selects this one from the chapter on other people's perfect children. 'I asked the teacher if there were any areas of weakness with Melanie (name changed) that we should be working on. She replied: "No, you have given me a little diamond and all I have to do is polish it."'

The Guardian

Welsh cab driver Tony Jones dressed up as Santa Claus every Christmas in Llanelli. But in December 2003 officials banned his white beard because he didn't look like his identity badge.

Daily Mirror

'We remain quite bewildered by the West Berkshire Youth Court verdict in the case of the 13-year-old girl convicted of drink driving on Christmas Day – a one-year supervision order and a two-year

driving ban. We suppose it's something that she won't be back behind the wheel again till she's 15.'
Guardian Diary

'Women are pretending to be men. Men are donning frocks and falsies. It's that time of year for the slapstick and buffoonery of a uniquely British entertainment – pantomime. Our continental and transatlantic cousins express utter bemusement... and that's just the way we like it. The most enduring appeal of pantomime is that there is something for everyone... the booing and hissing, the groan-inducing jokes, unfortunate innuendo, unmemorable songs, and awkward rhyming couplets.

**It is the peculiar nature of the British
To love panto, whatever your fetish'
From a *Times* leader**

Santa Claus is alive and well and living in Surrey. Researchers from EuroDirect found him there – along with two Jesus Christs, one in West Yorkshire and the other in Lancashire.
The Times

What better way of celebrating the season of goodwill than to gather together 4,250 runners dressed as Santa Claus to raise thousands of pounds for charity? But after taking part in the two-and-a-half mile fun run in Newtown, Powys, some of the Father Christmases headed straight

for the pub. It all ended up with more than 30 drunken men slugging it out in the main street. Police officers used CS spray and drew their batons to break up the fighting. Five men were arrested and four officers suffered minor injuries. PC Gareth Slaymaker confirmed that many of those involved were still wearing their Santa outfits.

The Times/Daily Mail

Have yourself a very merry Christmas... in a Britain where alcohol consumption rises by 41 per cent during December, drink-driving deaths rise by 18 per cent, murders rise by 4.2 per cent, and burglaries by 1.8 per cent. Suicides, however, drop by 7.9 per cent. Statistics compiled by the Policy Exchange think tank.

Daily Telegraph

The Royal Society for the Prevention of Accidents also revealed some festive figures:

- More than 6,000 people were taken to hospital on 25 December 2003.
- Over the 12 days of Christmas the estimated number of casualties rose to 80,000.
- The most common injuries were people stabbing themselves rushing to open – or wrap – presents.
- A mass of bruises and broken limbs were suffered by children falling off rocking

horses or new bikes, and by people falling
while putting up Christmas cards.
- Tinsel caused a large number of cuts and
Christmas-tree lights accounted for some
350 emergency admissions. *Guardian*

A £6.25 Fortnum & Mason Christmas pudding was
the present from the Queen to each of the 1,450
members of the Royal Household in 2004. One of
them got the sack after he put his pudding up for
auction on eBay with a £20 reserve price.

Daily Mail

'The Crown Inn – why not celebrate Christmas with us?
(Every day except Christmas and Boxing Day)'.
Ad in *The Leamington & Mid Warwickshire Review*
spotted by Dorothy Sharman.

Family gatherings at Christmas can easily go wrong –
even among the Royals. The Queen came a cropper
on Christmas Day 2004 when she stood up during a
meal. A flunkey pulled her chair away, thinking she
had finished. So, when she went to sit down again,
the Queen fell on top of her Corgis which, as usual,
were sniffing around waiting for titbits from Her
Majesty. The junior footman responsible was
mortified, but the Royals burst out laughing. Even the
Queen thought it was hilarious, said a palace source.

Sun

At least the royal Corgis did not face the danger of meeting up with Princess Anne's 'lethal English bull terrier, Florence'. At the 2003 festive gathering at Sandringham Florence attacked Pharos, the Queen's oldest corgi, with fatal results. At the 2004 event the Princess Royal's favourite pets were not on the invitation list.

Sunday Telegraph

Chapter 26

Odds and Sods

'Make It In Scotland' T-shirts made in Morocco...

Has anyone done an analysis between the relationship between junk mail and world events? Before the (Iraq) war, I was inundated by offers to enlarge my penis. This has now fallen off.

Letter to the *Guardian*

In the age of the couch potato, the television remote control was voted the best battery-powered invention of all time – beating the smoke alarm, radio and mobile phone. The personal vibrator, sixth in the top ten, was ahead of the laptop computer and the torch.

The Times

A reader writes from Somerset about her four-year-old grandson walking past a stout lady and saying: 'Coo, aren't you fat?' When told to apologise, he said: 'I'm sorry you're fat.'

Daily Mail

A Bedford couple named Peacock christened their baby son Drew and thought it was a lovely name until Mr Peacock did an Internet search on names. He got a shock when the search engine asked him: 'Do you mean Droopy C**k?'.

Sun

Bill Mellor of Leyland, Lancashire, rang Royal Mail about a parcel that had gone missing. He was told not to send his complaint form by mail 'because they get lost in the post'. Royal Mail called this an isolated case and promised compensation.

Daily Mail

J. Bilsby, of Chester-le-Street, Durham, recalls a colleague who lost his dentures down the loo. He called the local water treatment plant and they invited him to view some of the many strange objects that turn up in their filters – many of them false teeth. He not only found his own false teeth, but another set which fitted him perfectly.

Daily Mail

A woman who was due to give a talk called 'Follow me, I know where I am going' failed to turn up at Woodmanstern Women's Institute. She had got lost.

> Seen in the *Epsom Guardian*
> by Richard Owen of Epsom

Daily Mail readers reported some bizarre wrong number 'conversations'. Margaret Jones, of Shrewsbury, reported answering the phone to have someone totally unknown to her shout furiously: 'We think you're bloody ignorant and none of us will come to the wedding'. The phone was then slammed down.

> **Daily Mail**

A *Reader's Digest* poll named Tommy Cooper as the nation's all-time favourite comic. Comedian Bernard Manning said of him: "He could reduce a room to hysterics simply by standing up. People were laughing before he opened his mouth. Tommy had incomparable comic ability and, from anyone else, his one-liners might have seemed childishly simple":

- 'My friend drowned in a bowl of muesli. He was pulled in by a strong currant.'
- 'What do you give a cannibal who is late for dinner? The cold shoulder.'
- 'Two aerials meet on a roof, fall in love and get married. The ceremony was brilliant but the reception was rubbish.'

- 'I went to buy some camouflage trousers but couldn't find any.'
- 'Police arrested two kids. One was drinking battery acid, the other was eating fireworks. They charged one and let the other off.'

Daily Mail

'When I wanted a *Guardian* in the Highlands the shopkeeper asked: "Do you want today's or yesterday's?" "Today's," I replied. "Ah, ye need tae come back tomorrow then."

Letter from David Windridge,
Nuneaton, to the *Guardian*

A survey revealed that the contents of a woman's handbag could be worth hundreds of pounds. This prompted a letter to the *Daily Telegraph* from Irene Banahan of Leicester. 'A former police constable told me that when he attended road accidents a woman's first words were, invariably: "Where's my handbag?" not "How's my husband?"'

When John Hayzelden, Tring, Hertfordshire, went to buy linoleum he asked for a piece 6ft 6in wide and 14ft 4in long and was told: 'All measurements are in metres.' In that case, he said, 2m wide and 4m 40cm long. He was then told: 'We don't do that size precisely. It goes up in intervals of three inches at a time.'

Sunday Telegraph

The Times reader Mr B.H. Parker asked a Lowestoft supplier for 18ft of copper and was told: 'No, mate. We've gone metric. I can do you six metres. Do you want half-inch or three-quarters?'

The National Lottery website records some oddball facts about its winners.
They include:

- A man was walking under a tree when a bird pooped on him. He remembered that this was supposed to bring luck. He won £24 on a scratchcard. The same thing happened the following week and he won £444. He now regularly stands under the tree waiting for his lucky bird to perform.
- Billy Gibbons renamed his chicken 'Lucky' after it trod on its owner's calculator, selecting five winning Lotto numbers. 'Lucky' now helps Billy pick his Lotto numbers every Saturday morning.
- Tucking lottery tickets into underwear is the top favourite way of keeping them safe. (27 per cent of women keep tickets in their bra.) Other favourite places are: under the floorboards, taped to the body, in a Bible, in the microwave and under 'M' for millionaire in a dictionary.

The Times reader Quentin Howard tells of moving into a new house and asking for its telephone number to be changed to his name. He told the BT operator he did not want a telephone directory entry. He then asked what his telephone number would be and was told: 'I'm sorry, sir, we cannot give out ex-directory numbers.'

The Times

Pound coins are going missing at the rate of 39,000 a day. £300 million has disappeared since they were introduced in April 1983. Piled on top of each other they would stand 587 miles high. Liverpool Victoria Friendly Society report, quoted in *The Times*.

A string of reader's letters appeared in *The Times* about how much money there is to be found dropped in the street. One lady wrote about the excitement enjoyed by her husband when he found money like this. She said her son 'once laid a trail of pennies for him on the way back from the station. Rarely has he come home more joyful.'

The Royal Festival Hall in London is removing 118 seats to make room for audience members who are believed to have grown an average 1.5 inches in height – and probably more in girth – since the hall opened in 1951.

The Times

The desire of Michael Winner, 68-year-old film director, food critic and bon viveur, to become Mayor of London capsized in a sea of bureaucracy. 'What we have to do is send people to get ten signatures in 33 London boroughs (several of which I have never heard of). I have a staff of six, but I can't send them all out. I mean, who would be there to do the garden?'

Daily Mail

In a flurry of stories about celebrities giving their children 'silly' names, a Sunday Telegraph reader wrote: 'It is an old tradition. I traced a crest on a Victorian gun case and found that the owner was a Coffin who named his daughter Pine.'

Linda Atkins from Wincobank, Sheffield, spent ten days getting up a 1,000-name petition protesting against the closure of a local Post Office. She posted it to the Royal Mail by recorded delivery – but it got lost in the post. The Royal Mail's apology arrived along with a book of 12 stamps as compensation. 'It added insult to injury,' said Linda.

Daily Mirror / Sun

The Scottish quango Make It In Scotland has T-shirts made in Morocco.

Independent on Sunday

Prime Minister's wife Cherie Blair made headlines when she bought a 99p second-hand Winnie the Pooh alarm clock on eBay for her son Leo. Every day eBay receives ten million bids and accounts for a third of all British Internet traffic. Transactions have included:

- An 18-year-old Bristol University student auctioned her virginity, received 400 bids and accepted one of £8,400.
- One man sold his soul for £11.61. He promised to send the buyer an ownership document.
- A Margaret Thatcher handbag sold for £103,000.
- Christina Aguilera's used bathwater and thong fetched £810. *Daily Mail*

Former *Times* sub-editor Bill Bryson, who made his name writing humorous travel books, won a top prize for his science book *A Short History of Nearly Everything*.

The *Sun* printed a list of facts gleaned from the book, including:

- Modern humans have been around for only 0.0001 per cent of Earth's history.
- Every time a man thinks about sex, his hair grows.

Royal Mail watchdog Postwatch has complained that 49 packs of its campaign to 'Stamp Out Misdelivered Mail' were lost in the post. Linda McCord, a Postwatch regional manager, said: 'If it wasn't so serious, it would be funny.'

Daily Telegraph

The *I Love Books* Internet chat show asked people to have a go at condensing their favourite novels into 25 words or less. Among the ones selected by *Reader's Digest* were:

- *Three Sisters* by Anton Chekov: 'Three Russian sisters want to go to Moscow. They don't go.'
- *The Wizard of Oz* by L. Frank Baum: 'Transported to a surreal landscape, a young girl kills the first woman she meets, then teams up with three complete strangers to kill again.'

There are three types of economist: Those who can add up and those who can't.

Financial Times

The lavatories at the 2004 Glastonbury festival took their usual battering and fans were soon turning up their noses. But not Sir Paul McCartney, who had his own five-star facilities brought in for himself and wife Heather.

Sun

An acquaintance needed some books to put in a new display unit. I volunteered to buy some for her and inquired about her taste. She replied: 'Green – to match the carpet.'

Jackie Warden, Leyburn, North Yorkshire,
The Times

A hotel in Birmingham had a bookcase with shelves full of apparent classics. But only the bindings were genuine – the pages were blank. I wondered whether one bought such collections by the yard to fill up available space?

Brian P. Moss, Tamworth, Staffordshire, *The Times*

For 150 years generations of postmen delivered more than the day's mail to the villagers of Singleton in Lancashire. They were happy to take along vital supplies like bread, milk and pet food to the isolated residents. Not any more. The Royal Mail's time and motion men have decreed that the old traditions of this Domesday village (population 300) must be cast aside. Mrs Ivy Poole, 81, summed up the village's feelings: 'Whoever's done this is a rotter.' Two days later the *Daily Telegraph* reported that the Royal Mail had lifted the ban on the postman delivering groceries.

Singleton village has other singular traditions. By decree it can have only a single shop, a single inn and a single farrier.

Daily Telegraph

West Yorkshire's *Ilkley Gazette* reveals that two senior Royal Mail staff agreed to attend a village meeting to face furious complaints about late and misdirected deliveries. Unfortunately the RM officials were late and the meeting had to start without them. They had gone to the wrong address.

Indiana Jones star Harrison Ford ditched his action-man screen image to take a holiday on a canal boat cruising the waterways of Shropshire. The *Sun* dug deep to find ten exciting things about the county. Among them were:

- **Martin Wood, the town crier of Shrewsbury, is the tallest in the world – 7ft 2ins.**
- **Gingerbread men come from Market Drayton.**
- **Shropshire is home to the British Hedgehog Preservation Society.**

The Hayward Tyler Lutonia is the Rolls Royce of flushing lavatory cisterns. When Michael O'Brien's Lutonia failed to flush after 115 years the makers agreed to repair it – even though the Luton-based engineering company has not made flush lavatories for 70 years. They scoured their factories across the world but failed to find any Lutonia spare parts, so they sent an engineer to Mr O'Brien's semi in Luton. He took the worn-out bits and set about recreating a small piece of Victorian technology, involving technical drawings, mild steel implants and some advanced cast-iron welding techniques. The job took two weeks and cost £500. Mr O'Brien's Lutonia now flushes 'as good as the day it was made' – and he was not charged for the repair.

The Times

Andy Smurthwaite, 54, from Torquay, complained to his holiday tour representative that their hotel in Bulgaria had cockroaches in the damp bedrooms, broken glass in the swimming pool and smelly toilets which wouldn't flush. The tour rep responded by inviting Andy to come outside for a fight.

Daily Mail

In 1988, to the relief of many, Walls stopped printing jokes on its ice-cream sticks. In 2004 they reintroduced them, but dropped such groaningly unfunny oldies as:

Q: What lies quivering at the bottom of the sea?
A: A nervous wreck.
But this one remains:
Q: What is a mermaid?
A: deep she-fish. *Daily Mail*

Two brothers – Patrick Kerrison, 17 and Patrick Rico, 20 – who had tried to locate each other through the Salvation Army and the Internet finally found each other – working on the same building site in Plymouth. They discovered by chance that they were sitting side-by-side while on a tea break.

The Times

Have you heard the one about the academics who spent four days at taxpayers' expense pondering the profundities of why people tell stories beginning: 'Have you heard the one about...'? The University of Wales played host to the 2004 meeting of the International Society for Contemporary Legend Research, whose members try to figure out the origins and attractions of urban myths.

Robert Matthews in the *Sunday Telegraph*

Matthews went on to claim that one reason the public believes urban myths is because many of them are true. He then explained why in two out of every three trips to a supermarket, your queue will be beaten by one of the queues on either side of yours. And why the place you're looking for in the road atlas is usually in the awkward bits along the edges or down the central crease.

The story about Charlie Chaplin secretly entering – and losing – a Chaplin lookalike contest is often dismissed as an urban myth. It got another outing in the *Guardian* Weekend magazine in July 2004 and is confirmed on various websites.

Director Sam Mendes wrote in the *Daily Telegraph* that he had had a residence in Oxfordshire since 1992 and was not new to the area. Christopher Peachy, of Cirencester, Gloucestershire responded: 'Sam Mendes is way out if he thinks that 12 years residency qualifies him as 'not new'. My family came to Gloucestershire in 1891, but are still regarded as mere blow-ins by neighbouring farmers whose ancestors were active in this area in 1600.'

Daily Telegraph

English Heritage wants to resurrect the role of the jester after an absence of more than 350 years. It advertised: 'Jester Wanted. Must be mirthful and prepared to work summer weekends in 2005. Must have own outfit (with bells). Bladder on stick provided if required.'

Independent

'Morden has seen everything, from mammoths in the Ice Age, to being a region of forest and swamp with bears, boars and wild cats, to the quick development following the opening of Morden Underground in the swinging 1920s.'

Merton Council's magazine reported in the *Guardian*

A bag of rubbish being displayed as a work of art at the Tate Britain gallery was thrown out by a cleaner. Although German artist Gustav Metzger easily produced another bag of rubbish it was reported that an offer has been made to compensate him.

Independent

The *Sunday Mercury* reports how a Birmingham man was asked to cough up £1.21 in an incorrect postage surcharge if he wished to receive an unspecified letter. He paid the fee only to discover that not only was the envelope clearly marked 'Royal Mail. Postage Paid' but it contained an unsolicited letter offering a Post Office loan.

Guardian

Guardian readers know what they want. After some correspondence involving mathematics and philosophy (the complexities of which need not bother us here), Copland Smith of Manchester pleaded for the letters page 'to return to the simplicity of sandals and Marmite jars'.

European Council Directive 91/628/EEC provides cattle with a more comfortable train ride than that often suffered by people on British trains. The directive states that small calves must have 15cm between them when being transported by rail. David Wheatley, of Hanbury, tells *The Times* of his journey from Birmingham to Bromsgrove when there were about 100 people standing in a train comprised of two crowded coaches. Mr Wheatley points out that Article 5, Section 2 (g) of the directive also says the transporter must ensure 'that the animals are transported without delay to their destination'.

The Times

Amateur Bill Foggitt's weather forecasting often beat the Met Office at its own game. When he died, aged 91, in September 2004 practically every newspaper in the land carried obituaries. He and his family, from Thirsk, Yorkshire, had been keeping weather records since 1830. Bill studied wildlife to help produce his forecasts and one of his finest moments came in 1985 when the Met Office predicted a long cold spell. Bill contradicted this after seeing a mole poke its nose through the snow.

Yorkshire Post/Sunday Times

Stuart Rose, chief executive of troubled Marks & Spencer, was fighting to put the famous store back in the number one slot in 2004. But he did not please Sterling Murray, of Enfield, who wrote to the *Daily Telegraph*: 'He wore a Richard James suit and Thomas Pink shirt for one meeting and Connelly trousers and a Hermes tie for another. If he won't wear an M&S suit, trousers or tie, then why should I or anyone else?'

Sylvia Crookes, of Bainbridge, Wensleydale, emailed her Internet bank to tell them she had forgotten her password. The bank's help desk said that to get a new password she must enter her existing password. Two weeks later Sylvia wrote that her bank had 'taken £25 from me for being overdrawn. I am overdrawn because I could not get into my account to move money, because I didn't have a password.'

The Times

A book called *Crap Towns* named Luton as the crappiest town in Britain, but the entry that caused most surprise was Windsor as the second crappiest. One view that helped the affluent royal town to this unwelcome award was: 'Townsfolk believe that by living near the castle, they are more or less royalty themselves.'

Guardian

Sky TV's programme on some of the worst decisions of all time included:

- The nine publishing firms who rejected the first Harry Potter book.
- Alan Williams, the manager who turned down the Beatles.
- Record company boss who sold Elvis to RCA for a paltry $35,000. *Sun*

A book, the *Lore of Averages* by Karen Farrington, says:

- People sleep for 220,000 hours during a lifetime – that's 25 years.
- We spend 90 per cent of our time indoors.
- Sexual foreplay lasts 12 minutes.
- Wallpapering causes 400 people a day to go to hospital for treatment.

Eric James of London SE11 writes of the time when he was chaplain of Trinity College, Cambridge, in the 1950s. In conversation with Professor C.S. Lewis, he mentioned that he was due to 'make that dreadful journey to Oxford'. Lewis said: 'Dreadful journey? What do you mean? Before you depart from Cambridge, ring up the station restaurant at Bletchley, and ask them to put an omelette on a low gas when they see the Cambridge train approaching – as they do for Professor Lewis. By the time you arrive it will be done to a turn; and you will have ample time to consume it before you make your way to the Oxford train.'

The Times

In June 2004 it was reported that the number of mobile phones in use in Britain had risen to 56.2 million and soon there will be more mobiles than people. The current population is 60 million.

Sun

The inventor of the mobile phone, ex-RAF electronics engineer John Edwards, 64, said a Midland Bank manager in Merseyside refused him a start-up loan, saying: 'They'll never catch on. People won't want to carry a phone around with them.' Edwards got the loan from Barclays and is now a millionaire.

Sun

Alongside this story, under the headline 'Twits of Our Time', the *Sun* remembered how:

- **Decca turned down the Beatles in 1962.**
- **Twenty top firms snubbed James Dyson's revolutionary vacuum cleaner.**
- ***The Wind in the Willows* was originally rejected by publishers.**
- **Burt Reynolds blew his chance to play the first 007.**

Helen Ranson's publishing business relies on mail order so she arranged to collect her own post from the local sorting office in Hertfordshire. She was staggered to receive a bill for £2,600 from Royal Mail for providing a 'bespoke collection arrangement'.

Daily Telegraph

A squatter who lived in a rundown house in trendy Hampstead for 20 years has sold it for £710,000.

Daily Star

Following reports on the vast amounts of money paid to consultants by the government, two *Daily Telegraph* readers wrote:

- A management consultant used to be described as someone who borrows your watch and then tells you the time. Ken Stamper. Wirral.
- Someone who knows 100 ways to make love – but doesn't know any women. Roy Brazier, Greenford, Middlesex.

An IQ test has been devised for babies as young as six months. Questions include how well baby plays at pat-a-cake, this little piggy, stacking bricks and using a toy telephone. A mother trying out the test for the *Daily Telegraph* wrote that her baby would have made a much higher score if points had been available for 'ability to roll naked on the floor, pee on the carpet and be sick on at least five different outfits per day.'

No.10 asked former trades union leader Rodney Bickerstaffe to draw up a guest list for a reception for curmudgeonly transport union legend Jack Jones. Bickerstaffe showed Jones the list and Jack crossed out so many names that Rodney said: 'There's only going to be me and you at this party.' Jack replied: 'I haven't invited you yet.'

Daily Mail

Rail passengers have wasted more than 11,000 years on delayed trains since the railways were privatised eight years ago reported *The Times* in February 2005.

- 1,119,000,000 passengers suffered delays (almost equal to the population of China).
- 11,282 person-years equals the time that has elapsed since the last woolly mammoth.
- During that time the Old Stone Age ended, there was the Ice Age and wild dogs were domesticated.

Hamleys toy shop in London named the £80 Robosapien the 2004 toy of the year. It breaks wind and burps.

The Times

Demands for the settlement of bills in the sum of £0.00 are a constant source of fury. Geoffrey Mott, of Grays Inn Chambers, London WC1, tells of a friend who ignored such a demand from a book club. Increasingly threatening demands followed – and ceased only when, in desperation, he sent a cheque for £0.00.

The Times

2004 was the bicentenary of the Royal Horticultural Society and passionate British gardeners were able to wallow among a rich variety of literature available at an exhibition at the British Museum. This included an 1898 bestseller containing the immortal line by

Countess von Armin: 'The longer I live, the greater is my respect and affections for manure in all its forms.'

Telegraph Gardening

Six out of ten British women have so little confidence in men's DIY skills that they do it themselves. An insurance company survey also found a quarter of them have banned their chaps from undertaking DIY.

The Times

Following a story about tourists visiting the Sistine Chapel and asking for the locations of the other 15 chapels, a *Times* reader told of a relative who used to speak of having crossed the Seventh Bridge. When asked where the other six were, he said he didn't know – except that the Fourth Bridge was just outside Edinburgh.

The Times

Guides to some of Britain's top attractions have been telling the *Sun* about some of the daft questions tourists ask:

- **At Stonehenge: 'Where do you keep the stones at night?'**
- **At King's College, Cambridge: 'How do your choir boys hit the high notes? Do you still castrate them?'**

- At Edinburgh Castle: 'What time does the one o'clock gun fire?'
- In Scotland: 'What time are the Northern Lights switched on?'

The National Lottery celebrated its tenth anniversary in 2004:

- Wales' biggest Lottery winner, Mary Jones, 62, of Bala, Gwynedd, scooped a £9 million jackpot, but went on working as a cinema usherette. She said: 'After 24 years I still get excited every time the lights go down.' *Daily Mirror*
- Mel Eddison still carried on running his Manchester-based pallet-making firm after winning £2.5 million. He said: 'To me the business is like a hobby. I love it. I would pay to do it.' *Daily Mirror*
- Doug Wood won £2.65 million in 1996 and devoted himself to two ambitions: to visit every racecourse in Britain and to spend all the winnings on good causes and friends. He died in July 2003 with only £80,000 left – and one racecourse short of his target.

Independent

It was in 1999 that the brave members of the Women's Institute up in the Rylstone branch of the Women's Institute posed naked for a charity calendar. Since then hundreds have copied their initiative – ranging from rugby clubs and cathedral choirs to firemen and university students. It has all got too much for organisations representing Britain's 25,000 naturists who would like to see an end to the trend. It is, they say, giving nudity a bad name.

Sunday Telegraph

It's time to say goodbye to 'Legs Eleven'. They confuse the younger players now being attracted to the ancient game of bingo, which dates back to 1530. Traditional bingo lingo such as 'Kelly's Eye', 'Clickety Click' and 'Two Fat Ladies' makes the game look old-fashioned, say today's more professional players. They want the numbers completely straight – with callers referring to the four examples above as 11 1, 66 and 88.

Sunday Telegraph

Eat your heart out, Venice. Birmingham is to offer champagne gondola trips along its waterways. Landmarks include the International Convention Centre and the leafy suburbs of Edgbaston. Local worthies boast that Brum has more canals than Venice.

Daily Telegraph

While viewing a rather grand house my wife was delighted to overhear a lady assuring her friends that the grounds were designed by Calamity Brown. W. G. Cullis, Worcester.

The Times

Charles Dickens was arrogant. Winston Churchill was pigheaded. These are the conclusions of graphologists who studied the writing of famous people, including monarchs, philosophers and politicians. Henry VIII's writing revealed his attention-seeking nature and moodiness. Karl Marx was a difficult man who refused to listen in an argument.

Sunday Telegraph

Between 1824 and 1968 British theatre was controlled by censorship. Under the dictate of the Lord Chamberlain's office, all new plays were read for unfavourable or corrupting content with the intention of protecting the 'vulnerable' audiences of the time. The *Sunday Times* reports on a new book called *The Lord Chamberlain Regrets* which reveals that one work was censored in case it might offend Adolf Hitler.

Sunday Times

In the small Somerset village of Nunney, 82-year-old retired teacher Richard Lewis delighted locals with his writings, which included novels, poetry and some

271

history. Then he produced a work of fiction about the village which was not the twee tale of idyllic rural life that some villagers might have expected. The book, *A Fool in the Country*, included a man-hungry member of the Women's Institute "with the figure of a full-breasted swan", an adulterous policeman, a lady whose favours were available for the price of a packet of Woodbines and a hunky meter man "with thighs like a rugby forward", whose activities went beyond simple meter reading. Unfortunately, it was claimed, some of the characters bore resemblances to real residents. Mr Lewis was upset by the ill-feeling stirred up – and withdrew the book after selling only six of the 500 self-published copies. 'I fear people have read too much into it,' he said. 'I am now keeping a low profile.'

The Times

John Commins of Horsham, West Sussex, rang his two-and-a-half-year-old grandson to ask if he had seen the snow. But there had been no snow where the boy lived and Mr Commins promised he would bag some up and deliver it to him. However, the grandfather told the *Daily Mail*, 'I was ill for a week and didn't get to him. The next week it snowed in the boy's area and he rushed around the house shouting: "Grandad's been! Grandad's been!"'

The village of Bassingbourn in Cambridgeshire has selected the monument it feels best captures the essence of its rich and varied past – a £10,000, 5ft statue of a pile of poo – in memory of Victorian miners who dug up fossilised dinosaur dung for fertiliser.

Guardian/Daily Telegraph

A St George's flag is one of the top ten things most likely to deter a prospective buyer when viewing a house. Other turn-offs include:

- Pebbledash/stone cladding
- Concreted-over garden
- Over-enthusiastic Christmas lighting
- Garden gnomes. *Property Finder/ Daily Telegraph*

A boy's family have asked if they could please have his tennis ball back, almost a century after he lost it behind ornamental moulding at Lincoln Cathedral. It has been there, out of reach, ever since. But scaffolding is being erected during a cathedral cleaning operation and it is possible that Gilbert Bell's lost ball could be retrieved 'within the next decade'.

The Times

Cleaners at the Arches nightclub in Glasgow scrubbed the ladies toilet from top to bottom after finding it in a filthy condition. Later they learned that the soap stuck to the walls, the toilet paper littering the floor and the stains on the tiled walls were part of a work of art by artist Angela Bartram.

Daily Record/The Times

Essex, butt of a thousand derogatory jokes, has launched a campaign to rid itself of its vulgar image. It wants to change the perception that it is synonymous with brainless blondes devoted to sex and shopping. Unfortunately, fate often finds a way of kicking the county in the teeth. A 14th-century skeleton discovered there turned out to be that of a girl with syphilis – the earliest example known in Europe.

Daily Telegraph

When the *Times* posed the question 'What is the oldest recorded joke?' one reader submitted this one, believed to go back about 2,000 years:
Cicero sees a slave in Rome who looks exactly like himself. 'Ho, slave,' he says. 'Was thy mother ever in Rome?' 'No, master,' replies the slave. 'But my father was.' Peter Nicholson, London N6.

The Times

The joke about the barber who asks 'How would you like your haircut, sir?' and is told: 'In silence' has got hairs on it. It is in a jestbook compiled by the Spanish playwright Juan Timoneda who died in 1583.

John Wardroper, London N1, *Observer*

While playing hide-and-seek, Donna Fawley's three-year-old son climbed into a suitcase and pulled down the lid. The combination lock engaged and Mrs Fawley could not remember the combination. She had to drill air holes into the suitcase and get the Manchester fire brigade to release the boy.

Daily Mail

The new £300,000 post office at Wrexham lacked a vital amenity – no letterbox. Royal Mail promised to install one immediately.

Sunday Telegraph

Mrs R. Minshull of Berkshire submits extracts purportedly from genuine letters to the Inland Revenue:

- 'Please send me a claim form as I have had a baby. I had one before, but it got dirty and I burnt it.'
- 'I have not been living with my husband for several years and have much pleasure in enclosing his last will and testament.'
- 'I cannot pay the full amount at the moment as my husband is in hospital. As soon as I can I will send on the remains.'

- 'I have to inform you that my mother-in-law passed away after receiving your form. Thank you.' *Daily Mail*

More than 8,000 items have gone missing from the British Library since 1997. They included a collection by the Roman poet Horace, printed in 1540 – and rare copies of the *Dandy* and *Beano*.

Daily Telegraph

People advertising in personal columns often insist that they want to meet someone with a GSOH. But what does it mean? A survey reveals that for a woman a Good Sense of Humour means someone who makes her laugh. For a man it means someone who laughs at his jokes.

The Times

Randall Riding comes from a family of gamekeepers and remembers his grandfather's way of dealing with poachers. He filled shotgun cartridge cases with rice and salt, saying: 'The rice only takes the skin off their backsides, but the salt stings like hell.'

Daily Telegraph

The advice Russia gave its spies in London was hardly the stuff of James Bond. A 1939 Red Army intelligence guide says that hotels like the Ritz, the Dorchester and the Savoy are frequented only by people with the necessary social standing, so it is always advisable to arrive at hotels with smart luggage... 'The British spend a lot of money on good luggage.' If being followed, dodge into places like Harrods, Selfridges or the Science Museum – they have many exits.

Good places for rendezvous are the Peter Pan statue in Kensington Gardens, the bus stop outside Gloucester Road tube station, the Old Oak Tea Rooms in Pinner and the bandstand in Hendon Public Park.

Join the AA – they will represent you for any petty motoring offences, thus avoiding personal contact with the police.

Guardian/Daily Telegraph

Nelson had a broad Norfolk accent that made him sound like Bernard 'Bootiful' Matthews.

Daily Telegraph

'It's a myth that *Just William* is a rebel without a cause. His world is safe and secure... with cooks and nannies, big houses, croquet lawns and tennis clubs. The joke is not that William is kicking against his middle-class upbringing, but that we know he will follow his father into the City and will court Violet Elizabeth Bott at the tennis club dance.'

Simon Hoggart, *Guardian*

Two weeks in the Mediterranean exposes you to as much sun as a year in the UK.

Independent on Sunday

When she was three, Mrs C.M. Wood's daughter, of Cheltenham, was given her first helium-filled balloon. On arriving home she let go of the string and said: 'I've dropped it on the ceiling.'

Daily Mail

A study found that men were better than women at coping with technology-based products. Overall men outscored women 104 to 97. No need for smugness, though – 14-year-olds scored 117.

The Times

The commonest house name in Britain is Rose Cottage, followed by Woodlands, Sunnyside, Orchard House, Hillside, Hillcrest, Orchard Cottage, Meadow View, Wayside and Holly Cottage. Dunroamin didn't make the top ten.

The Times

Professor Richard Wiseman challenged an investment analyst, a financial astrologer and a four-year-old girl to select shares that would improve over a year. The child won.

Guardian